THE MARRIAGE SEED

How to Cultivate the Relationship You Desire and Deserve

By: Lionel Moses

Copyright ©2024

All rights reserved.

No part of this book may be used or reproduced in any manner without the publisher's express written permission, except for using brief quotations in a book review.

Paperback ISBN 979-8-9897662-0-8

eBook ISBN 979-8-9897662-1-5

Published By: Lionel Moses www.lionelmoses.com

Dedication

To my parents, James and Earlene. Your life provided me with a picture of a great marriage. I learned from your examples and the love you shared.

To family, friends, loved ones, and mentors, thank you for helping me learn the values of relationships.

Table of Contents

Introduction 1

Chapter 1: Survey The Ground - The Foundation 13

Chapter 2: Germination Time 37

Chapter 3: Purposeful Singleness 48

Chapter 4: Once Upon a Time 71

Chapter 5: Faith: Act As If It Will Grow 91

Chapter 6: Germination - In the Beginning 116

Chapter 7: The Big Cover-up 125

Chapter 8: Active Blooms 140

Chapter 9: We Have Been Doing It All Wrong! 154

Chapter 10: Fertilize: Drop the F-bomb! 171

Chapter 11: Fertilize it! 201

Chapter 12: What's In the Soil? 210

Chapter 13: Ranks & Strategy 220

Chapter 14: The Strategy - Seed, Bury, Water, and Grow 243

Chapter 15: Licenses and Authority 254

Conclusion: Plow 262

INTRODUCTION

Have you ever felt like your relationships are not reaching their full potential? Do you need help figuring out why?

Relationships are challenging and require work, but we must understand the proper work to do for them to bloom. Just as a seed planted has different needs, relationships thrive when given what they need.

What are those needs? That's what we're going to explore in our time together.

I believe in each relationship's potential. We are relational, so when we thrive, our relationships thrive, pure and simple. The idea of a healthy relationship still exists; it's simply the perception of relationships that needs to change.

Introduction

In life, we often encounter the profound truth that what we seek frequently arrives in the form of seed rather than in a state of maturity. This principle resonates deeply in relationships, where the initial sparks between two individuals set the stage for a union. In life, a sperm cell meets an ovulating egg, and the journey of existence begins—a blend of joy, restlessness, compromise, and the unpredictable beauty of new beginnings.

Imagine this complex process as a metaphor for the way many of us enter the world. I invite you to explore this process in the following pages—a journey to understand the art of "seed sorting" in relationships. This book is not just about deciphering relationship data or facts but about delving into the very essence of compatibility—the seeds that, when planted, determine the fruits of our connections.

Like a vast garden, the dating landscape offers tools like Bumble, E Harmony, Facebook Dating, Plenty of Fish, Match, Christian Mingle, and Upward, all designed to take a scientific approach to finding a compatible partner. Yet, no matter the algorithm, these tools rely on the accuracy of the data entered. If the seed, the initial information, is

Introduction

flawed, the resulting compatibility will inevitably mirror those inaccuracies.

> *Seed selection in relationships is a meticulous process that requires time and attention.*

Much like my experience during Desert Storm in 1991, where unforeseen circumstances affected my thought processes and emotional responses, the true nature of a seed often reveals itself over time. Only through seasons of shared joy and hardship can one discern the fruits and wounds a relationship may bear.

Many of the principles in this book are from my personal experiences. Like many others, I haven't had the pleasure of finding, courting, and marrying my soulmate or life-mate on my first attempt. I've had a few long-term relationships, including two marriages, and one thing I learned along the way is that there is always room for improvement. But I think the best skill I learned was to assess myself. Through many conversations within my relationships, whether personal, professional, or intimate, I have learned that my perspective is not the only one. Thus, you can't have a successful relationship without

Introduction

factoring in human experience. Here is a gem you can try before diving into the book. Practice saying "I'm sorry" and "I apologize." Those four words can change the trajectory of a failing relationship- but only to do it if you genuinely mean it.

I write not as a scholar or a specialist but as one who wears the wounds and scars of mistakes. Yet, one who has the joy of knowing that a fun-filled, satisfying, and thriving loving relationship is possible, which means possible for me! Before embarking on a relationship, the objective is to understand myself and clarify what doesn't work for me; at that crossroads is where the seed of a successful relationship lies.

In our fast-paced world, putting oneself first often influences how we connect with others; therefore, knowing the difference between what we genuinely need and prefer is essential. While physical attraction can start a relationship, shared life philosophies are the building blocks for a lasting connection. While most social media platforms, movies, television, and other forms of entertainment focus on surface-level attractions, genuine relationships require a deep understanding of each other's needs and a commitment to shared values. It's about going

Introduction

beyond the surface, addressing root causes, and embracing the things that make a relationship work. A healthy seed, with proper care, produces a healthy plant.

Just as I discovered the impact of my experiences on my emotional well-being, this book encourages you to embark on a journey of self-discovery. How can we expect others to relate to our inner selves if we are unaware of our complexities?

Your emotional health is the cornerstone of a healthy relationship. You pave the way for a genuine connection by addressing and understanding your seed. Remember that assessing our seeds is an act of profound self-love and love for others.

So, as you embark on this exploration of seed sorting, remember that the first seed you must assess is the one within yourself. Doing so enhances your emotional well-being and creates fertile ground for authentic and lasting connections, the essence of the seed-sorting journey—a journey toward wholeness and love.

Introduction

Here are a few common misunderstandings about relationships:

- Love Alone is Enough: Many believe love is enough to sustain a relationship, but it's only the foundation. Like a plant, a relationship needs trust, communication, and mutual respect to thrive. Trust is the soil that provides stability, communication is the water that keeps the connection strong, and mutual respect is the sunlight that helps it grow. Even the strongest love can wither without these elements, just as a seed will fail without proper care. For a relationship to blossom, love must be nurtured with effort and intention.
- Conflict Means the Relationship is Failing: Conflict is often seen as a sign of failure in a relationship, but it's an opportunity for growth. Just as rain nourishes plants and helps them grow stronger, healthy conflict can deepen understanding and strengthen a relationship's roots. When approached constructively, disagreements allow partners to address issues and refine their bond, like a gardener removing weeds after a storm. Couples who work

Introduction

through conflict build resilience and trust, ensuring their connection grows sturdier instead of being uprooted by challenges.

- Your Partner Should Complete You: A healthy relationship involves two whole individuals who complement each other. Expecting a partner to "complete" you is like planting a seed and expecting it to grow without proper care. Each person is like a separate plant with its roots. Strong relationships thrive when two healthy individuals grow side by side, not when one depends entirely on the other. Both partners can contribute equally by focusing on personal growth, self-awareness, and self-care, creating a balanced and thriving partnership.

- Saying "it's not my fault" in a marriage deflects responsibility and halts progress, much like neglecting a wilting plant. A healthy relationship requires both partners to take ownership of their role in challenges. Blaming others or external factors ignores the need for nurturing and care. Growth in marriage, like with plants, happens when both partners address issues together. By asking, "How can I help fix this?" instead of

Introduction

shifting blame, you foster accountability and cooperation, creating an environment where the relationship can thrive. Ignoring problems or avoiding responsibility stunts growth, just as neglecting a plant leads to its decline.

> *Avoiding responsibility with phrases like "it's not my fault" hinders personal growth and makes relational growth impossible.*

Addressing common misconceptions in relationships, such as "it's not my fault," challenges individuals to take responsibility for their actions, a rarity in many societies. The success of the relationship is the responsibility of both partners. While the specific incident may not be your fault, maintaining the relationship is your responsibility. Before I go further, let's be clear: even in a relationship, there must be boundaries. Boundaries are things that are put in place to protect the emotional and physical well-being of each individual. We will talk more about boundaries later in the book.

Taking the "it's not my fault" approach in relationships is generally unproductive. In a marital relationship, taking

Introduction

responsibility means actively addressing challenges and contributing to the partnership's growth, like a programmer debugging or refining their code to align with the programming language's rules. Similarly, a garden involves recognizing when care is lacking—such as watering or weeding—and taking steps to nurture it.

Like following the hierarchy in programming, relationships benefit from adhering to a structured approach and acknowledging and correcting deviations to ensure a purposeful journey. A relationship's intricate coding requires attention to detail, recognition of errors, and appropriate responses to foster growth and progression. By embracing a structured approach and accepting responsibility for our actions, we contribute to the harmony and success of our relationships. A healthier approach is to ask, "How can we address this together?"

Life follows a similar pattern: A man and a woman meet, sparks fly, and they unite in "unity." Just like a sperm cell meets an ovulating egg, life begins. Mom eats, baby eats, both are restless, and nine months later, the baby joins the world amid whatever mom and dad have to go on.

Introduction

Using this simple yet oversimplified illustration, I will provide principles in this book to help you establish thought patterns for making better relational decisions. As a father and now a grandfather, I've often said apologetically to my children and others, "Kids do not come with instructions." The truth is, neither does relational seed sorting.

What does seed sorting have to do with relationships? To that, I would say everything! When a man and a woman meet, they gather data. This data-gathering phase is what I refer to as seed sorting. I chose the term "seed" because similar data will produce the same type of fruit when planted like seeds of the same sort.

Enter the concept of "The Marriage Seed," which introduces the idea of seed sorting. When two people meet, the information collected becomes the foundation for intelligent relationship decisions. The dating process involves this critical seed sorting, ensuring the proper foundation for a compatible relationship.

However, selecting the proper foundation can be challenging, stressing the importance of timing. Personal experiences can significantly affect our thoughts and

Introduction

feelings, highlighting the need to assess foundations during various seasons to understand what a relationship might grow into. Start this evaluation by looking within, understanding, and evaluating your emotions. Emotional well-being is crucial for a healthy relationship.

So, when someone advises against settling in a relationship, ask, "How's your seed?" Prioritizing your emotional well-being sets the stage for a healthy and meaningful connection. Taking the time to explore and understand your emotions helps to ensure a solid foundation for the growth and success of a relationship. You can't expect someone else to relate to the inner person you don't know. That was an area that I failed in! I entered marriage with a lot of emotional baggage because I didn't know myself! As we take this journey, you will learn that I do not make excuses for things I have done that are wrong. However, I have learned that you can't grow beyond your current state without acknowledging why something happened, which is a first step toward fixing.

Wisdom and knowledge are required for your seed to grow to its full potential. Growth doesn't occur by accident; it requires intentionality. I must remind myself: How can I find someone to love me if I don't know and accept myself?

Introduction

I must know its type to properly care for the relational seed within me; this will dictate the care and nourishment required for my relationship's maximum potential.

We're going to explore these concepts deeply together. Are you ready to go on a journey with me?

> *Welcome to a transformative odyssey where the seeds of self-awareness and emotional health catalyze a fulfilling and enduring relationship. Let's begin!*

CHAPTER 1:
SURVEY THE GROUND - THE FOUNDATION

It was a beautiful June day when we finally closed the deal on our first home together. We were surprised by the house, which looked pretty different from the pictures online and in the realtor brochures.

After several months in our home, autumn arrived. Autumn is my favorite season because the trees are already beautiful from the various colors, making the scenery even more stunning as the leaves fall. I learned that a leaf's true colors become visible in the fall due to less sunlight and reduced groundwater.

In the summer, plants perform photosynthesis, turning water and carbon dioxide into oxygen and sugar using light. Chlorophyll, a plant chemical, makes photosynthesis happen and gives plants a green color.

Before the leaves fall, something significant happens. With less light, there's a big change in the trees. When light decreases, things start to fail and fall. However, it's not just the leaves; those troublesome acorns fall, too! They ended up all over my flower beds, the lush grass I worked hard on all summer, the sidewalk, and the driveway. Now, I see my lovely shade trees a bit differently. How can such a beautiful tree, which made me love the green outdoors in the summer and provided excellent shade, become such a nuisance?

While picking up those acorns was no fun, I got excited, knowing that every moment can be a teaching opportunity. Regularly raking or using my new backpack leaf blower, I couldn't handle all the fallen acorns. I tried blasting them with the leaf blower at full power, but some acorns had rooted themselves. I kept blowing, but because the acorn seeds had established a root system, they stuck around, and now mulch was scattered everywhere. I hadn't planned on replacing the mulch, but the roots of the acorns made the mulch more susceptible to the leaf blower than the seed with roots.

While cleaning up and trying to save some mulch for later, I noticed something interesting: Two acorns had joined together and started sprouting.

At that moment, it dawned on me that many things, like our lives, relationships, and marriages, start as simple seeds. If you plant a seed, something will grow. What other things begin that way? All plant life starts with a seed, and all life does. Life begins when a father and a mother, a male and a female, come together and plant the seed. The same goes for a strong relationship!

THE MARITAL FOUNDATION

Solid roots are the foundation on which a plant or tree thrives. For example, marriage is tall and enduring when founded on a solid foundation. Picture the foundation as the bedrock of a relationship, providing stability and resilience against the inevitable storms. Just as a building's foundation determines its strength, the foundation of marriage dictates its ability to weather challenges. Consider the metaphor of a skyscraper—it reaches significant heights only because its foundation is meticulously planned and robust.

Survey The Ground - The Foundation

In relationships, the foundation symbolizes the shared values, mutual understanding, and emotional connection between partners. A deep dive into this metaphor reveals that the strength of the structure corresponds directly to the care invested in its initial stages. It's not just the external aspects; it's also the internal fortitude that keeps the marital relationship.

When counseling individuals contemplating marriage, I always suggest they see everything honestly. Lack of honesty destroys trust. Lack of honesty in a relationship is like noticing weeds in a garden or flower bed while not pulling them out. When preparing the soil for seed, it is best to remove all weeds. Weeds grow aggressively. If not removed, weeds will take over your garden. Here's another metaphor- ignoring weeds in your garden is like pouring a foundation and accepting that it's only a couple of millimeters off. I am not saying to rip out everything and apply weed killer; that may prohibit the seeds from germinating properly. Neither am I suggesting that you break up all of the poor foundations and start afresh.

I'm saying, be wise; anything found on the foundational level will impact every subsequent level. As with the weeds, pull it up at the root and identify it.

Survey The Ground - The Foundation

Weeds represent things that naturally grow in a particular environment. Weeds will grow with little to no effort, yet they feed off the nutrients you give to your plants. In a relationship, identify the things that tend to reduce or choke the life out of your relationship naturally. Once identified, make an intentional effort to remove the root cause.

With a poured foundation, if the area is small enough, you can shave it to spec and continue building without damaging the integrity of the future structure.

> *In the grand narrative of marriage, the foundation acts as the bedrock upon which the entire structure rests.*

Consider this foundational layer a carefully painted canvas on which the intricacies of love, trust, and understanding intertwine. Like the concrete and steel that support a building, a solid foundation in marriage ensures stability and resilience.

Just as builders meticulously plan and lay the groundwork for a structure that can withstand external pressures, couples must nurture the foundational elements to fortify their relationship against life's inevitable storms. Building construction, gardening, and relationships require care but differ in approach. Construction relies on a solid, unchanging foundation to withstand external forces. Gardening thrives on ongoing care, adapting to changing conditions. Relationships, like gardens, grow through mutual effort, trust, and communication, evolving with time and challenges. All require attention, but true growth comes from nurturing and adapting together.

> *True growth comes from nurturing and adapting together.*

STABILITY AND RESILIENCE IN RELATIONSHIPS

Marriage is an ongoing construction project, with each partner contributing to the growth and development of the relationship. Note what I said—contributing to the growth and development of the relationship, not each other. We can't fix ourselves, much less another person. But if you have figured out how to create a solid relational foundation through a one-and-done task. Please share that with me! I have learned integrity is developed and proven within the relationship process. Relationships go through seasons; each comes with pulls, pushes, and twists. Relationships can only be sustained through the process. That process is understanding two keys. The first key is personal growth, which contributes to our relationship's growth and development. The second key we have already touched on is that individual growth processes differ.

Nonetheless, it's all part of the process. Using the building metaphor emphasizes that constructing a fulfilling marriage involves joint effort, continuous improvement, and a shared vision for the future.

Imagine a resilient building standing tall in the face of a storm, unmoved and unshaken. Similarly, stability and resilience become the cornerstones of a well-rounded marital relationship. When the foundation is solid, couples are better equipped to navigate challenges without compromising the integrity of their bond.

Understanding and fortifying the foundational elements of relationships allows couples to bounce back from setbacks, transforming challenges into opportunities for growth. The relationship's stability becomes a testament to the strength of the initial groundwork—a foundation crafted with intention, care, and a shared commitment to weathering the storms together.

THE POWER OF INTENTION

In marriage, the threads of intention weave the most patterns. Imagine intention as the architect's blueprint, the guiding plan that shapes the trajectory of a successful marriage. It's not merely about hoping for the best; it's about deliberately setting the course with positive energy and purposeful direction.

> *If you're not intentionally addressing an issue, you will certainly unintentionally neglect the problem.*

Most know neglect can leave your partner feeling tolerated and not treasured, which isn't great. We will discuss that later in the book. For now, we will focus on nurturing our garden through the power of intention.

Positive intentions are the seeds that germinate into the lush garden of a thriving marriage. When both partners approach the groundwork for building the relationship

Survey The Ground - The Foundation

with a harmonious attitude, they deliberately foster love, respect, and shared values. Positive intentions serve as the cornerstone, ensuring that every action, decision, and interaction stems from a place of goodwill and a commitment to mutual growth.

> *Just as an architect envisions a building's design before laying the foundation, couples must craft a blueprint for marriage.*

The marital blueprint involves thoughtful consideration of the values that will form the pillars of the relationship. Deliberate intentions go beyond momentary feelings; they embody a conscious choice to embark on a journey of love and understanding with a shared vision of what marriage can become.

Intentions find their true power when aligned with shared values. These shared principles become the guiding force, akin to a compass directing the marriage toward a purposeful destination. Good intentions coupled with the core values of both partners create a strong and resilient framework for the relationship.

Survey The Ground - The Foundation

Positive intentions set the tone for the entire relationship. When both partners consciously approach challenges with optimism, disagreements with understanding, and celebrations with shared joy, the marriage becomes a haven of positivity. It's not about avoiding difficulties but facing them with a united front fueled by the shared intention to overcome hurdles together. Intention is also about adopting a mindset of abundance in love and support. Instead of viewing the relationship through a lens of scarcity or competition, couples with positive intentions celebrate each other's successes, share in each other's joys, and create an environment where both can flourish. This mindset becomes the fertile ground where the seeds of a purposeful and fulfilling marriage take root.

In the context of marriage, intention is not a fleeting thought but a continuous thread that runs through every moment. It's a commitment to nurture, cherish, and invest in the relationship's growth. As couples embark on this intentional journey, they build a marriage and a legacy of love that stands the test of time.

DISCOVERING SELF: SELF-AWARENESS IN RELATIONSHIPS

In my former life, I worked as a corporate tax professional. I enjoyed reading tax laws and finding opportunities to save the company money. I loved the compliance side, where we would follow the rules of calculating the due taxes and reporting it to the proper authorities. Another aspect of the role that I enjoyed was being on the merger and acquisition team. We called it the M&A team. My role on the M&A team was performing due diligence analysis on companies my employer was looking to merge with or acquire. My due diligence analysis contained information based on the data provided about the financial health of a prospective company. Once we proved that the liabilities associated with joining the new company did not outweigh the potential benefits, moving forward with the merger or acquisitions was safe. Just as a builder meticulously studies the lay of the land before construction, individuals in relationships must turn their gaze inward. Understanding the intricacies of one's values, desires, and weaknesses sets the stage for a robust foundation. This self-exploration is not a one-time event but an ongoing process, much like surveying the landscape as it evolves.

Survey The Ground - The Foundation

Introspection becomes the blueprint of the self, a guide that allows individuals to navigate the complex terrain of their emotions, aspirations, and fears. Picture this as an architect carefully drafting plans before construction begins. Knowing oneself intimately is not about perfection but about acknowledging and embracing the contours of one's personality, forging a map for personal growth and shared evolution in a relationship.

Values are the pillars supporting the structure of our lives. As we delve into self-discovery, unveiling and understanding our values is crucial. Much like testing the soil to ensure it can withstand the weight of a building, identifying our values ensures that the relationship is grounded in shared principles. This process illuminates who we are and what we hold dear.

Desires act as the building blocks of our dreams, shaping the skyline of our aspirations. Self-discovery invites individuals to unearth these desires, laying them out like carefully chosen materials for constructing the shared future of a marriage. Recognizing and communicating these desires with a partner becomes the collaborative act of creating a vision that aligns with both individuals' dreams.

Survey The Ground - The Foundation

I grew up in an era where we played outside. I remember watching superheroes on television, whether animated or human. I just loved and desired to be a superhero. But I have always been a realist. So, I never desired to be Superman. I can't fly. But Batman was doable. Batman was a real guy who was creative and could fight. I desired to be the guy with resources to care for my relatives, keep my family's name great, and woo the lady I loved.

Self-discovery is about navigating these areas with honesty and humility. Just like trees and plants need reinforcements and sticks/posts tied to them to strengthen them, couples can fortify their relationship by acknowledging and addressing each other's vulnerabilities. It's an acknowledgment that weaknesses, when understood, become opportunities for growth rather than obstacles.

Self-discovery isn't a static process but a dynamic journey of growth. It's akin to an ongoing construction project where each revelation, every nuanced understanding of self, contributes to the evolving landscape of the relationship. Embracing personal growth ensures that the foundation remains sturdy, adapting to the changes that time and experiences inevitably bring.

Survey The Ground - The Foundation

Self-discovery establishes a shared language in a marriage's blueprint. Partners who understand their narratives can communicate more effectively, fostering an environment of empathy and mutual understanding. This shared language becomes the bridge between individuals, connecting their inner worlds and creating a harmonious space for cohabitation.

As individuals engage in the profound journey of discovering self, they contribute to the masterpiece that is their marriage. This process of introspection, understanding values, acknowledging desires, embracing weaknesses, and fostering growth becomes the artistic strokes that paint a canvas of shared experiences.

> *Ultimately, a marriage grounded in self-discovery is not merely a structure but a living, breathing masterpiece that stands the test of time.*

CHOOSING A COMPLEMENTARY PARTNER

Choosing a life partner is a profoundly important decision, and humility emerges as a guiding principle in this crucial endeavor. In relationships, humility becomes the cornerstone for recognizing personal strengths and, more importantly, acknowledging inherent weaknesses. Drawing parallels between the careful selection of materials in building construction and partner selection, we explore how humility sets the stage for a complementary partnership.

Humility is a virtue and part of a resilient marriage's root system. When individuals approach partner selection humbly, they become acutely aware of their limitations. This self-awareness helps them recognize the need for a partner who complements and fortifies areas of weakness. Consider this akin to a builder acknowledging the structural requirements of a building and choosing materials that compensate for vulnerabilities.

In pursuing a complementary partner, an honest assessment of personal weaknesses becomes imperative. Making an honest assessment of our shortcomings is not an exercise in self-deprecation but a courageous acknowledgment of areas where growth and support are needed. As builders choose materials that compensate for the limitations of others, individuals seek partners whose strengths offset their weaknesses, creating a synergy that contributes to the overall strength of the relationship.

Survey The Ground - The Foundation

Many people think I am weird, which may be accurate, but I love ensuring anyone in a relationship knows I am human and will blow some things up. Not intentionally, but it will happen. It is part of the human experience. Your actions may not be deliberate, but your unintentional acts will one day affect you and others. Know yourself, love yourself, and continue working to better yourself. It's part of the life cycle.

Analogous to constructing a building that can withstand diverse challenges, a complementary partner complements both strengths and weaknesses. A complementary partnership doesn't imply finding someone identical but rather someone whose qualities align in a way that builds a balanced and resilient foundation. You should envision your ideal partnership as a collaborative construction project where each of you uniquely fortifies the structure.

Moving beyond idealized notions emphasizes the need for a practical approach to partner selection. The analogy here is choosing materials for a building project. Builders meticulously assess the properties of various materials to ensure compatibility, strength, and durability. Similarly, individuals should assess potential partners, considering their unique qualities that align with their aspirations and vulnerabilities.

Suppose you are an introvert and like time alone. Connecting with someone who is always the life of the party and thrives off being in the spotlight may cause challenges. If you are jealous and your partner is a networker and enjoys working a room for opportunities, watching your partner engage with others, speaking, smiling, laughing, and probably even sharing a physical touch or embrace may cause severe emotional discomfort and vulnerability. I am not saying that these differences are deal breakers. An honest assessment of whether the pain from the differences outweighs compatibility is necessary, and then an evaluation of how it compliments is essential.

In this journey of partner selection, humility serves as the blueprint for a complementary union.

> *The intentional recognition of one's need for support and the willingness to seek a partner who fulfills those needs lays the groundwork for a harmonious and enduring relationship.*

Humility is far from being a sign of weakness. Humility is a strength that contributes to the longevity and depth of the marital connection.

Humility is the cornerstone of recognizing personal weaknesses and acknowledging the need for a complementary partner. In relationships, humility involves a deep understanding that no one is perfect and realizing personal limitations are not a sign of weakness but strength. Much like an architect who recognizes the limits of materials and seeks to compensate for them, humility allows individuals to accept imperfections and actively pursue a partner whose strengths offset their weaknesses.

Humility says that I care and don't have all the answers. Humility also shows your partner that what they feel, think, and desire matters. It also says that I am willing to be your student in this space. Many times, I have found that operating in humility leads to greater intimacy. Communicating gives space for your loved one to fill in the gap. That is crucial to a healthy relationship. We can't think of another. Humility is when we come alongside our partner, intimately sharing our weakness of not knowing. Leave the void for them to fill while loving them where they are.

Humility also plays a crucial role in fostering effective communication, a key ingredient in any successful relationship. Couples who humbly approach each other better navigate challenges and conflicts, viewing the challenges as opportunities for mutual growth rather than threats to the relationship's stability. In essence, humility becomes the adhesive that binds two individuals, creating a bond that withstands the test of time.

PRACTICAL APPROACH TO PARTNER SELECTION

Many times in our lives, we discover the truth in things we hear as a child. While I never spoke of marriage as a child, and the adults in my family did not discuss their relationships, they shared wisdom about both. Much of the knowledge they shared came from stories with multi-dimensional principles. I learned that principles are laws that work if you work them; if you don't, there will be a corresponding result.

My Grandma would say things like, "You catch more bees with honey." I grew up in the city, and we didn't harvest honey; grandma would swat at it if there were a bee. So, I wondered, what's this about catching bees? Contrary to popular belief, sometimes we can know too much. In other words, the answer to our problem is often before us, and we overlook it due to its simplicity. We do the same thing when picking partners. Many times, our approach isn't practical. We often spend more time looking for traits and characteristics that we like instead of looking for complementary characteristics and attributes. The traits we like will keep our attention for a short time. However, the complementary characteristics will make creating a life together easier. The good thing is we deserve both. But most relationships begin based on likes. If you like someone, you ask them out. That was easy. Well, sometimes it is. Identifying what you want is usually straightforward and typical. What we are going to discuss is choosing your complementary partner.

CHOOSING A COMPLEMENTARY PARTNER

Choosing a complementary partner involves a practical, intentional approach that mirrors seed planting and gardening. This process requires deliberate research. About the soil type you have, the climate, exposure to the sun, etc.

Survey The Ground - The Foundation

Assessing Strengths:

Individuals should begin by identifying their strengths and acknowledging the unique qualities they bring to the relationship.

Understanding personal strengths allows for intentional choices that contribute to the partnership's overall strength, similar to selecting robust materials for construction.

Recognizing Weaknesses:

Humility is essential as individuals assess their weaknesses, recognizing areas where they may need support or complementary qualities.

Understanding these weaknesses positions individuals to actively seek a partner whose strengths fill these gaps, creating a holistic and resilient foundation.

Seeking Complementary Qualities

In the same way, builders select materials that complement each other for structural stability. Individuals should seek partners whose qualities enhance the overall dynamics of the relationship.

We should look for complementary qualities in our relationships, such as thoughtful consideration of shared values and life goals and the ability to work harmoniously towards a shared vision.

Striking a Balance

Like flourishing gardens, successful partnerships emerge from carefully planting seeds with unique attributes.

> *Cultivating a thriving relationship requires a mindful approach, akin to sowing seeds in fertile soil that will nurture the growth of a beautiful garden.*

In marriage, humility and self-denial are vital nutrients for the seeds of love. Just as a gardener tends to the needs of each plant, operating in humility and self-denial becomes like food that fortifies unity within the relationship. The willingness to let go of personal desires for the greater good of the relationship becomes the rich soil that supports the roots of a resilient partnership. Forsaking personal desires is like navigating through the intricate paths of a garden, carefully tending to each plant's unique needs. It involves transcending individual wants for the collective benefit of the relationship—an acknowledgment that the journey of love is not always a straightforward path but a rich one where humility and self-denial illuminate the way.

Recognize that relationships, like seeds, require intentional care and attention—plant seeds of love, understanding, and shared experiences to guarantee a strong foundation for growth. One of the beauties of seeds is they tend to reproduce after their kind. Suppose you plant the seed of love and nurture that seed. Guess what will grow? You got it. Love will grow. Acknowledge the significance of the foundational moments in your relationships.

Celebrate milestones and the start of your journey together, reinforcing the importance of shared beginnings. We recognize that a successful relationship commences with deliberate and positive intentions. I can't overemphasize the importance of self-awareness in constructing a healthy relationship. I invite you, the readers, to reflect on your values, desires, and vulnerabilities. Only then will you be prepared to discover a complementary partner—a humble approach that acknowledges personal weaknesses, goals, and strengths.

Choosing a complementary spouse involves finding someone whose strengths balance your weaknesses and whose values, goals, and character align with yours. Look for a partner who shares your core beliefs, communicates effectively, and supports your growth while challenging you to improve. A complementary spouse brings harmony by celebrating differences and working together to build a strong, unified relationship.

CHAPTER 2: GERMINATION TIME

The initial inspiration for this book came from a day spent outdoors doing yard work. When I'm in the yard, I feel peace and tranquility in the ambient sounds and stillness of nature. Nature fosters a connection with God and underscores the significance of life. When connected to nature, I feel alive!

The second source of inspiration concerning the bonds within relationships arose from observing my youngest daughter and my oldest granddaughter playing in the backyard. Even though they had hula hoops, ropes, scooters, and dolls, they weren't playing with them- they were playing with the acorn seeds on the ground, and now and again, they would find something fascinating to tell Dad and Granddad. One of their most notable finds was an acorn with two seeds growing together as one. I had never seen two seeds sprout together. Observing the two seeds sprout together made me think of marriage and how two people come together as one to create something beautiful. There were several unique things about those two acorns growing together. Two distinct entities converge, creating something beautiful.

First, it's important to remember that even though there's one root, there are two separate acorns. I wondered: Did they share a leaf in the previous season? Had they been on the same branch? Were they from the same tree- or the same type of oak tree? Does it matter? When these seeds connected in the ground, their shells were flexible even though they started as two separate seeds with shells.

Individual seeds can't create a joint root. The shells gave way to the co-seed, and the exposure that weakened them allowed them to do something that might seem unusual. Almost every seed that falls to the ground has the potential to grow into an oak tree. The soil condition where they land makes some more apt to sprouting.

Germination Time

For a healthy marriage, you need two essential things: 1. getting the proper nutrients and 2. being in a place that helps you grow. No matter how good or how much love you share, there will always be challenges (like soil in a garden). This soil breaks down the protective shell you had during your single days. If the soil is dry, it takes longer to break open the shell. So, rain or dew comes in, moistens the shell, and makes it vulnerable while covering it with soil to expose what's inside. This phase is called germination. The germination of a seed happens before everyone sees it in the sunlight.

> *Relationships are like seedlings; they thrive in the right environment.*

We only know what's in us once we go through different seasons. It's essential to accept the challenging times (the dirt/rough times) and the rainy times because they will come and are necessary for growth.

I will discuss the essential nutrients that keep a relationship healthy and lasting. Let's examine some of these nutrients and see what they can teach us.

COMMUNICATION

Communication is the heartbeat of a successful relationship. This vital nutrient allows understanding and empathy to flow, forming a solid base for a thriving relationship. With good communication, you'll avoid encountering the same problems. Communication is what builds intimacy, strength, and understanding between two people. Who wants a relationship without intimacy? I sure don't! When I talk about intimacy, I'm not referring to sex. I mean emotional closeness, having a strong bond, and sharing a sense of togetherness and friendship. These qualities naturally build a deeper connection, making us feel supported and understood.

Authentic Expression means being open and honest about your thoughts, feelings, and dreams. It's having the courage to share your vulnerabilities to create trust and intimacy. I've learned that most internal frustrations come from withholding my authentic expressions. Everyone wants to experience love for who they are.

Active Listening: It's not just hearing words but understanding the emotions and intentions behind them. It's about creating a space where your partner feels heard and valued. This mutual exchange builds a deep emotional connection.

Consistency: Regular, open conversations are key to effective communication. Commit to ongoing dialogue that strengthens your relationship over time. Perspectives shift as life changes, so sharing how and why we adjust is important to keep the connection strong. Date nights are a great way to reconnect and deepen your understanding of each other.

Honesty is the Cornerstone: Being willing to express thoughts, even when uncomfortable, creates an environment of transparency and builds trust. Relationships thrive when partners commit to being honest about their feelings and thoughts- building a foundation for trust and open communication without fear of judgment.

TRUST

Trust goes beyond believing in your partner's honesty. It's the confidence that you can rely on each other emotionally, mentally, and in vulnerable moments. Trust is the foundation for real intimacy; it creates a safe space for both partners to be themselves. Building and maintaining trust is an ongoing process that requires effort from both parties. It involves open communication, active listening, and understanding the importance of trust in the relationship.

RESPECT

Respect is about genuinely valuing and appreciating your partner every day- not just on special occasions. Kindness, sweet gestures, and caring words make your partner feel loved. Everyone has a unique way of experiencing love. In his book, *The Five Love Languages*,

Gary Chapman labels how one experiences and shows love "love languages." It's important to note that the language used to show love may not be the same language that makes you feel loved. These love languages include gift-giving, words of affirmation, physical touch, acts of service, and quality time. Recognizing your partner's love language can enhance communication and deepen your relationship. Learn their love language and express yourself in ways that resonate with them. Respect also means accepting your differences and being each other's biggest supporter. It's not just saying, "I support you," but showing it through actions—like standing by them as they chase their dreams and celebrating their victories.

> *Patience is understanding that all relational growth takes time.*

PATIENCE

It's acknowledging that building a solid relationship is a gradual process. Patience connects the present to the future, recognizing that personal and relational transformation happens gradually. It means giving each other space to grow. Patience encourages personal exploration, allowing each partner to pursue their passions and become the best version of themselves.

Patience also plays a crucial role in navigating mistakes. It's about understanding that errors are not roadblocks but stepping stones to growth. Patience creates a compassionate space where forgiveness and understanding replace blame, fostering an environment that brings healing and growth. We are patient with others because there is an area in our lives in which we need someone to be patient with us. Consider it a grace plant. We give grace because we will one day need to reap grace and patience.

Even with all the right ingredients for a healthy relationship, they will only work in the right environment. Let's explore the critical aspects of the ideal environment for your relationships to bloom into their full potential.

FERTILE SOIL (FOUNDATION)

Think of the core of any meaningful relationship as soil—a blend of shared values, common goals, and mutual understanding. This soil is the fertile ground from which the roots of a strong connection can grow. Shared values, like seeds planted in this soil, represent the fundamental principles and beliefs both individuals bring to the relationship. They are an agreement on what matters and your shared goals, forming the bedrock of your relationship.

Decision-making is the process that builds this foundation. Collaborative decision-making establishes equality and unity, shaping your relationship one decision at a time. The commitment to growth, both individually and in your relationship, acts like the nurturing sunlight and rain, ensuring the flourishing of this foundational soil.

RAIN (ADVERSITY)

> *Facing challenges together is an opportunity for growth in a relationship.*

Challenges, whether financial difficulties, health issues, or external pressures, allow you to stand against the storm and become stronger together. In moments of shared adversity, the roots of the relationship dig deeper into the foundational soil. These challenges can fortify rather than weaken the relationship. The rain becomes a source of nourishment, prompting the relationship to absorb lessons, adapt, and emerge stronger. How does that occur? Outwardly, like rain, it is harder to see while driving. Rain also makes you consider the attire that you wear. If you're like me, there are some clothes you don't want to get wet, and your footwear must be appropriate for the weather. Inwardly, or unseen by the normal eyes, that soft, muddy terrain softens the earth so the roots can grow deeper.

SUN (JOY AND CELEBRATION)

Joy is crucial in a relationship. It's not just about celebrating big wins; it's about finding happiness in everyday moments. Sharing joy builds memories that fuel your happiness, creating a positive atmosphere and strengthening your bond. The shared laughter, warmth, and simple pleasure of doing things together embody joy—the essence of what makes your relationship meaningful. The sun enhances the relational nutrients of trust and respect.

DEW (RENEWAL)

Regular refreshment and spiritual connection are essential in any relationship. This gentle dew revitalizes the bond, encouraging continuous growth and evolution. Renewal manifests through intentional engagement in activities that breathe life into your connection. It's about breaking the routine and committing to rejuvenation, whether starting a new hobby or embarking on an adventure together. Your deliberate effort becomes the dew that quenches the relationship's thirst for vitality, signifying an ongoing commitment to its well-being.

The right environment involves accepting challenges and joys, embracing effective communication, trust, respect, and patience, incorporating the nutrients of a healthy relationship, and creating an environment that promotes growth. We need to remember that the very first relationship we have is one with ourselves. Before successfully applying the nutrients required for a healthy relationship with anyone else, you must successfully manage those nutrients in your singleness.

CHAPTER 3: PURPOSEFUL SINGLENESS

As a skilled gardener plants a seed, individuals must purposefully sow the seed of a meaningful connection during their season of singleness.

Purposeful singleness points towards an individual on a profound journey of self-discovery, encouraging them to venture into the depths of their desires, values, and aspirations. Purposeful singleness allows individuals to unravel the layers of their identity, understanding the intricacies that make them unique. This self-awareness becomes the base upon which a future relationship has the proper nutrients to grow.

As I write this book, I am in the season of purposeful singleness. I was married; I have children and even grandchildren. Yet, I am learning so much about myself. Before I go any further, I must clarify that a season of purposeful singleness is not for the faint of heart! I am grateful for my personality and the ability to laugh at myself. Here I am, at the ripe age of fifty-plus, embarking on a journey of self-discovery- but you don't care about that. You need to know that I have adult children with families, and Pop Pop is learning more about himself every day. I shared that so you don't think it's too late. It's not!

WHAT I'VE LEARNED ABOUT ME

I've learned that it is okay to have fun, that God never intended or expected me to be perfect, and that it's OK not to like something everyone else does. That's what makes me unique.

I am analytical and results-oriented by nature. That was a blessing for me, and it came with a not-so-great backside. I have excelled in my career and business endeavors because of my ability to analyze a situation quickly and lay out an effective resolution. I am allowing my creative mind to help build my financial legacy. The blessing was that growth came quickly, but there's a backside. I became more intellectual and creative with my development but had few opportunities to work with my hands. I love working with my hands! Purposeful singleness offers an expansive period for personal growth. Embrace this time to flourish individually by developing your skills, nurturing your talents, and refining your character. Like the carefully laid bricks that shape the base of a building, these experiences contribute to your individuality, making you a multifaceted and invaluable partner in relationships.

The purposeful single life involves skillfully preparing the soil for the seeds of companionship. Part of the soil preparation process entails understanding your relationship contributions and what you seek in a partner. It's about cultivating emotional intelligence, honing practical communication skills, and embracing the art of compromise – essential elements that serve as nutrients to nurture the budding relationship connection. In this preparatory phase, the ground becomes fertile and richly textured, ready to receive the seeds that will eventually sprout into a flourishing and resilient relationship. The beauty of a seed is that seeds germinate. Seed germination is when a seed develops into a new plant, beginning with sprouting a root and shoot. It requires the right conditions, such as water, warmth, and oxygen, to take root and grow.

Purposeful Singleness

In a relationship, **germination** represents the initial stages of connection and commitment.

The key is having the nutrients in the soil before planting.

I have a lovely lawn—that was a brag. My secret is that while many people focus on feeding their grass, I focus on keeping the proper micro and macronutrients in my soil. I care more about the root system than the grass blades.

Approaching purposeful singleness with a strategy involves envisioning a shared future with a partner and proactively cultivating the attributes that will contribute to a thriving companionship. You do this by fostering patience, resilience, and empathy, all qualities that fortify a relationship.

As we engage in purposeful singleness, we aren't just building for ourselves but co-creating a solid foundation for the shared journey that awaits a relationship.

EMBRACING PERSONAL GROWTH: CULTIVATING RESILIENCE AND EMBRACING CHANGE

The call to embrace personal growth is a resounding anthem, echoing the transformative power of resilience and the wisdom to navigate change. This Chapter is a testament to the notion that individuals can undergo a metamorphosis within the cocoon of self-discovery, emerging not only more robust and more adaptable but simply better.

Purposeful singleness invites individuals to cultivate resilience. Much like the seasons that shape the landscape, life's journey is fraught with challenges. The cornerstone of personal resilience is the ability to bounce back from setbacks, learn from experiences, and adapt to adversity.

> *This period of singleness serves as the forging ground, where the fires of life's trials refine and fortify the inner strength needed for a lasting relationship.*

Change is the only constant in life, and purposeful singleness is an opportune time to acknowledge this truth and welcome it with open arms.

Purposeful Singleness

Just as a seed faces the challenges of weather, soil conditions, and external factors, we must nurture our inner potential, allowing it to take root, flourish, and adapt to the ever-shifting circumstances of life. Embracing change during singleness means acknowledging personal growth as an ongoing process. It involves shedding old paradigms, unlearning limiting beliefs, and remaining open to the possibilities that change can bring to both individual and relational spheres.

Purposeful singleness is not a state of isolation but a dualism between independence and interdependence. In this phase, individuals learn to stand confidently on their own yet remain open to the collaborative moves of a future partner. It's about fostering individual strength without building impenetrable walls, recognizing that fulfilling relationships require partners to lead and follow in harmony.

I married my high school sweetheart. We had a good life together, but most of that life centered on our kids and family. At first glance, some may ask what is wrong with that. I would answer that question by saying we should prioritize our marital relationship above family and even our kids. Here is a quick and simple lesson. My children from that union are all adults with families of their own. Unfortunately, many relatives who influenced our marriage are no longer with us. If we had prioritized correctly, our relationship may have withstood the tests of time. Relationship prioritization is a lesson I learned; the seeds and signs of dysfunctional priorities are nutrients, which are now part of my relationship regimen. I look at myself and any potential partner for priorities that could be out of place.

Empathy, the ability to understand and share others' feelings, is the cornerstone of meaningful connections. It flourishes in the soil of personal growth. As individuals undergo their unique journeys, encountering diverse experiences and perspectives, their capacity for empathy expands. Empathy is pivotal to fostering deep and meaningful connections in relationships.

INTENTIONAL SELF-IMPROVEMENT

Purposeful singleness periods offer time and space to explore one's passions, interests, and values. Whether it's acquiring new skills, pursuing uncharted territories, or honing existing talents, self-discovery becomes an ever-expanding landscape rich with opportunities for personal growth.

One of the things that I am embracing on my self-improvement journey in singleness is accepting me for me. The adage that says you can't fix what you won't acknowledge is true. I enjoy working out in the gym because I want to live long, be healthy, and have an excellent quality of life. After all, I need to have the energy to enjoy my grandbabies. Ok. It's not a need, or is it? No one told me that at a certain age, your body changes without sending a memo. To maintain my body and physical strength, I hired a coach to tweak the exercise for maximum results and reduce the risk of injuries. A friend who is a bodybuilder is working with me on my diet. I shared this story so you know that self-improvement is beneficial, but having a coach, mentor, or partner is better.

At the heart of intentional self-improvement are clear and achievable goals for personal development. These goals act as compass points, guiding the growth trajectory and providing a sense of purpose whether the aim is professional advancement, academic pursuits, mastering a new skill, or pursuing personal goals.

CONTINUOUS LEARNING AND ADAPTABILITY

Individuals living a life of purposeful singleness recognize that growth is not confined to specific milestones but is a perpetual journey. Cultivating a love for learning, remaining curious about the world, and staying adaptable to change fosters a spirit of intellectual and emotional agility – qualities that resonate deeply in the realm of companionship.

Emotional intelligence is a cornerstone of intentional self-improvement. It refers to the ability to recognize, understand, manage, and influence emotions—one's own and others'. Emotional Intelligence involves empathizing with others and identifying, understanding, and managing emotions. Developing emotional intelligence improves communication, strengthens relationships, and enhances decision-making by fostering self-awareness, self-regulation, and empathy. Its benefits include reduced stress, better conflict resolution, and greater success in personal and professional life.

Emotional intelligence becomes the compass that guides individuals through the complex landscape of human emotions, facilitating deeper connections and effective communication within oneself and in future relationships.

That is why I recommend always maintaining the posture of a student—a student of life, others, and self. Self-improvement advocates for prioritizing physical, mental, spiritual, and emotional health. Cultivating healthy habits, fostering self-care routines, and nurturing resilience contribute to a robust foundation. Individuals learn that self-love and well-being are not selfish endeavors but prerequisites for offering genuine love and support to a partner. It's impossible to love someone else properly if you don't love yourself. And how can you truly love yourself if you don't know yourself?

THE INTENTIONAL CONNECTIONS

Intentional self-improvement does not unfold in isolation; it converges with mutual aspirations in purposeful singleness. Individuals recognize that their evolving selves should align with the shared vision they hope to create with a future partner. This intersection ensures that personal growth enhances individual lives and harmonizes with the collective narrative of meaningful relationships.

Can you see the importance of purposeful singleness? How can you genuinely align with another when you don't know yourself? Before going into the Navy, I worked as an auto mechanic. I went to school for it. Although I was not aware of it at the time, it was in automotive class that I had my first relationship. No, not the one with my high-school sweetheart, but the one that came as a result of working with my classmates to troubleshoot the problems on a car. Our teacher taught us how to diagnose issues on a vehicle. What he did was wrong! Unbeknownst to us, he had sabotaged the engines to see if we could work together before the end of the class. We could not accomplish the mission within the time constraints without our combined efforts. There were just too many systems for one person to check alone. Our collective knowledge and the ability to harmonize helped us to stay one of the top teams.

> *Purposeful singleness is a deliberate planting of seeds, where the careful sowing of intentional connections nurtures the growth of meaningful relationships.*

The act of planting intentional seeds goes beyond the scope of romantic pursuits. The process begins by cultivating a diverse social landscape encompassing meaningful friendships and mentorships. Much like a carefully planted seed, each connection contributes a unique element to the garden of personal growth. Purposeful singleness encourages individuals to explore connections of different ages, backgrounds, and perspectives, promoting a broader understanding of our world.

DISCERNING COMPATIBILITY THROUGH CONNECTIONS

Meaningful interactions provide invaluable insights into shared values, communication styles, and emotional resonance. Emotional resonance is the ability to deeply connect with and reflect another person's emotions, fostering empathy and understanding. Whether engaged in deep conversations, collaborative projects, or fun outings, purposeful connections become a litmus test for the compatibility that forms a relationship's bedrock. This discernment process aligns individual aspirations with the potential for mutual growth, ensuring that each step contributes to the rhythm of what should be a harmonious partnership.

My undergraduate degree is in Organizational Management, with a minor in Diversity and Inclusion. One of my favorite classes was World Religions. What fascinated me the most was how each group lived according to their respective belief systems while living within the same culture as others of different beliefs. With this new information, my relationship compatibility discerning process changed dramatically. I learned that diversity breeds perspective. Varying perspectives can breed better decisions, and better decisions can lead to better outcomes and connections.

> *Purposeful singleness introduces individuals to a myriad of perspectives.*

NAVIGATING THE DYNAMICS OF FRIENDSHIPS AND RELATIONSHIPS

Purposeful singleness is woven into relationships, from an acquaintance you've seen on occasion to the camaraderie of friends and the depth of romantic entanglements. While the types of relationships listed are not exhaustive, they provide a structure for identifying core relationship categories. It gives a choreographed sequence for navigating the dynamics of relationships.

Purposeful connections are not mere transactions; they are seeds planted in the fertile soil of shared experiences that contribute to growth. As the grand garden of purposeful singleness unfolds, intentional connections intersect with the individual's sense of purpose. This alignment ensures that social interactions contribute to personal growth and individual aspirations. Cultivating intentional connections becomes a harmonious process, planting the seeds of the solo pursuit of purpose and tending to the garden of shared connections that lay the foundation for companionship.

NAVIGATING CHALLENGES IN PURPOSEFUL SINGLENESS

Resilience within purposeful singleness extends beyond merely bouncing back from adversity; it's a dynamic force that propels individuals forward. This section broadens the understanding of resilience, portraying it as a versatile skill set rather than a reaction to hardship. Individuals are encouraged to view resilience as a proactive force that fosters adaptability, emotional intelligence, and a profound sense of self. By embracing resilience in this holistic sense, purposeful singleness becomes a transformative journey, with challenges viewed not as obstacles but as opportunities for growth.

In boot camp, we learned to walk in formation. The instructions were to start with your left foot. Doing so put us in sync while marching or walking in formation. However, there were times when your foot hit unstable ground. When that happened, you would lose your step and find that you needed to keep cadence with the rest of the company. Always start back on the left foot to keep cadence when you get off step. Yes, we all start at the same time, using the same foot, but when you encounter something unexpected in your path, you learn to adjust your steps to get back into cadence. It is possible! As individuals, we have to adapt to unique challenges.

Resilience and purposeful singleness are the ability to adapt to the changing rhythms of life. They involve navigating the unpredictable cadence of challenges and demonstrating flexibility in response to life's fluctuations. By developing an adaptable mindset, individuals can face uncertainties with a composed demeanor and adjust. This adaptability is not just a survival mechanism; it's a key instrument in orchestrating a purposeful solo journey that can seamlessly transition into a harmonious relationship.

Emotional resilience emphasizes the importance of understanding and managing one's emotions. It guides individuals through embracing vulnerability without succumbing to emotional turbulence. Emotional resilience becomes the melody that allows individuals to navigate the complexities of relationships with grace, fostering a deeper understanding of self and potential partners.

By weathering the storms of self-doubt and societal expectations, individuals emerge with a fortified sense of self. The ability to withstand external pressures and maintain authenticity becomes a skillful performance, setting the stage for genuine connections and the purposeful relationship you seek.

I am completing this book at one of the most preeminent times in my life- I lost my mother and dissolved my business within months of each other. I cannot articulate the grief associated with knowing my mother was ill and deciding that I needed to realign my life so that I could spend more time with her. I have no regrets!

However, having to walk away from my business after spending almost a year trying to find a buyer created significant external pressures and challenges. Did I mention that I was also newly divorced?

Yes, I was. After being divorced for two years, I should have been over the emotional strain. I was. Yet, when there were many life-directing experiences on the precipice for me, there were times when I experienced self-doubt regarding almost everything! After my divorce, I doubted my ability to make good decisions. Committing to a relationship, especially a long-term one like marriage, was a decision that I thought long and hard about before proposing. So, when the outcome wasn't as I expected, the seed of self-doubt grew. The good news is those experiences, encounters, and feelings are nothing more than life directors. Where you allow them to direct you is in your control. Fortified by their ability to navigate challenges, individuals emit a magnetic authenticity that attracts companions who appreciate their strength and character. In this context, resilience is the subtle undertone that enhances the melody of purposeful connections, ensuring that challenges encountered become stepping stones rather than stumbling blocks.

RESILIENCE AND PURPOSEFUL COMPANIONSHIP

Individuals who have weathered challenges and emerged resilient contribute to a companionship built on a solid foundation. The symphony reaches its pinnacle as resilience and purposeful companionship harmonize, creating a masterpiece.

The metaphorical symphony of purposeful singleness is a collective masterpiece, with everyone navigating their unique movements. Let's explore the nuances of emphasizing that resilience is not a solitary endeavor but a collaborative effort. Individuals are encouraged to appreciate the harmonies and dissonances of their solo journeys, recognizing that shared resilience contributes to more affluent and profound masterpieces of purposeful singleness.

Authenticity resonates as a central theme in intentional self-discovery during purposeful singleness.

Are you tired of hearing me talk about authenticity and intentionality? I sure hope not. Authenticity is a core element in all relationships.

I recall going to a homeopathic doctor for various allergen tests. I also wanted to discover the best foods based on my body type and lifestyle. Out of the blue, one day, the doctor pointed out that while I walk upright, I have a weak chest. First, let me say that I am human and a man. No man that I know wants to hear that they have a weak chest. She said I have a strong back that pulls my shoulders back to give me the appearance of a more developed chest. Did you catch that? My back made my chest look stronger. I knew the maximum weight that I could bench-press wasn't great. But I never really addressed it. It took a doctor consulting me to understand. I didn't want to hear that, but she didn't hurt my feelings. It's a good thing I had my emotions under control. This story informs you that my imbalanced musculoskeletal system didn't appear weak. In actual practice, I would compensate by using other muscles to support my weak chest muscles. Strengthening your authenticity will position you to see who you are and learn what truly complements you.

Intentional self-discovery directs individuals to inventory their passions. This process illustrates how purposeful singleness becomes an opportune time to explore and cultivate personal interests. Individuals amplify their richness of self by identifying and passionately pursuing their intrinsic desires. Reflective practices acknowledge growth, celebrate achievements, and embrace the ongoing journey of self-discovery. The symphony becomes a living narrative, resonating with the individual's continuous evolution.

VULNERABILITY AND AUTHENTICITY

Genuine authenticity emerges when individuals allow themselves to be seen in their entirety, embracing strengths and vulnerabilities. Growth gains momentum as individuals authentically express their thoughts, feelings, and aspirations, fostering an environment of openness and transparency. Cultivation becomes a transformative experience in purposeful singleness, creating genuine connections founded on sincerity.

Many have asked if I will ever marry again. The answer is a resounding yes! However, with that, yes, comes a lot of work on my part. One of the most important things I am addressing in this phase of purposeful singleness is allowing myself to be authentic and vulnerable. You may wonder what I mean by being vulnerable with myself. That is a very comprehensive question. Neither time nor ink in my proverbial pen will allow me to answer that here thoroughly. What I can do is help you to identify when you are not vulnerable with yourself. If you find yourself defending an inspiration, desire, or aspiration within your thought process, you may not be allowing yourself to be vulnerable. If you feel that you need to change for fear of not being accepted, you may not permit yourself to be authentic. These are examples of vulnerability's internal and emotional struggles, yet I must find a partner to complement me. Like most, I want a partner who genuinely loves me and provides a safe place to become vulnerable. A complementing partner is what most of us, including myself, desire; to get that, I need to allow that inner person to be exposed, even at the risk of rejection.

Vulnerability is a delicate sprout within the germination phase of purposeful singleness. Planting involves nurturing vulnerability to forge deeper connections. By embracing vulnerability, individuals engage in careful yet decisive cultivation that strengthens the roots of companionship. The process becomes an art form, with vulnerability as its delicate and transformative centerpiece.

Authenticity emerges as the lifeblood of connection in the growth of purposeful singleness. The root from a seed gains depth as individuals authentically present themselves, allowing the rhythm of authenticity to resonate with like-minded companions. The planting process becomes a dynamic exchange, with partners working harmoniously to sow the seeds of a flourishing connection. Purposeful singleness, seen through the lens of this planting, becomes a rewarding experience where individuals cultivate growth with grace and understanding.

If one practices purposeful singleness when they meet their partner, planting can organically become a shared endeavor, with both partners contributing to the growth. Collaborative cultivation portrays purposeful singleness as a joint planting where the unique contributions of each partner sow the seeds for a beautiful and evolving narrative.

THE FLOURISHING GARDEN OF PURPOSEFUL COMPANIONSHIP

Purposeful singleness is like a flourishing garden where intentional self-discovery plants the seeds for purposeful companionship. This movement illustrates how intentionally cultivating one's identity, values, and passions during purposeful singleness results in the blossoming of a vibrant garden. Purposeful companionship emerges as the flourishing flower of this garden, representing a union grounded in shared values, mutual understanding, and a commitment to growth.

The culmination becomes shared experiences, individual growth, vulnerability, and authenticity. Purposeful singleness and companionship are portrayed not as separate chapters but as interconnected elements in the overarching narrative of a fulfilling and purpose-driven life. Being purpose-driven in spouse selection is like planting a garden with clear goals, choosing the right seeds, and nurturing them to thrive. The relationship has a strong foundation when both partners share values and goals.

The narrative is dynamic but ever-evolving. Individuals, now companions, continue to grow, learn, and embrace the journey together. Purposeful companionship becomes a harmonious extension of purposeful singleness, with the shared melody echoing intentional choices, self-discovery, and authentic connections forged during the solo journey.

CHAPTER 4: ONCE UPON A TIME

Mid-flight to Fort Lauderdale for a sales convention, I yearned for my ex-wife. Memories of her infectious smile, our shared laughter, and my dreams of providing her with a fairy-tale life filled my thoughts. As John P. Kee's soulful "Never Shall Forget" played on my earbuds, I suddenly realized. In the initial stages of most relationships, there's a sense of euphoria where we believe we're on top of the world and everything is perfect. We meticulously plan a fairy-tale life, envisioning every detail we think will lead to the happiness we desire and deserve. However, this euphoria is often short-lived as we get to know our partner better, and their flaws and imperfections become apparent.

> *It's crucial to remember that no one is perfect, and every relationship will have its ups and downs.*

This phase can be challenging for many couples as they grapple with reconciling their idealized vision of their partner with the reality of who they are. It's crucial to remember that no one is perfect, and every relationship will have its ups and downs. Instead of forcing our partners into an idealized mold, we should focus on accepting them for who they are and working together to build a healthy relationship.

A practical way to achieve this is by focusing on shared values and goals. Identifying what's important and what we want to achieve together helps create a shared vision for the future. This approach keeps us focused on what truly matters and prevents us from being overwhelmed by day-to-day challenges.

To build a shared vision, we need open and honest conversations. Open conversations involve sharing our thoughts and feelings, even when difficult or uncomfortable, and being receptive to our partner's perspective. Openness to compromise is critical.

Once identified, shared values and goals can create a realistic, achievable, and measurable vision for the future. Regularly revisiting this shared vision ensures we stay on track and make progress.

Having a shared vision helps us stay focused on what matters and avoids getting bogged down in daily challenges. It lays the foundation for a robust, healthy relationship built on mutual respect, trust, and understanding.

Openness and honesty with our partners form the bedrock of effective communication, paving the way for trust and a deep connection. Effective communication involves sharing thoughts and feelings, even when challenging or uncomfortable.

Good communication is a two-way street. It's not just about expressing ourselves; it's equally about actively listening to our partner. Being fully present in the moment and giving our partner our undivided attention shows our commitment to understanding. Asking questions and seeking clarification when needed enriches the conversation.

Another crucial part of communication is being ready to compromise. Compromise means being open to different perspectives and finding common ground. Remember, we don't always have to agree, but it is vital to work together to find solutions that work for both of us.

Communication goes beyond words—nonverbal cues matter. Body language, tone of voice, and facial expressions play a role. Attention to these cues helps us better understand our partner's thoughts and feelings.

Try having regular talks. Pick a time to share what's on your mind and listen to what they say. Ask questions and be ready to find solutions. Doing this helps make relationships strong and happy. When faced with disagreements, work together to find solutions that benefit both of you. Working together strengthens your connection.

In the grand scheme of things, it's essential to recognize that relationships require work and effort. Building a strong and healthy relationship demands dedication and commitment from both partners. It means putting in the time and energy, especially when things get tough, and showcasing a shared commitment to making the relationship thrive.

She might express a vision of her ideal partner, someone standing between 6' and 6'4', possessing a physique that could make Adonis jealous. A man saved by grace, showering it upon others, understanding our occasional need for it. Intelligence and being grounded are a must – an intellectual worshipper. Financial freedom and abundance are not just goals but his way of life. Romance and passion come naturally, so he prefers watching a romantic movie with his queen over a sports championship game. It doesn't matter if the New York Jets defy the 3.86% odds and make it to the Super Bowl. Even if given free tickets, accommodations, airfare, and a $5,000 spending voucher for the Super Bowl, Mr. Right would choose the tearjerker if the Mrs. preferred. I haven't mastered this part yet; I'd probably start some heavy negotiations before conceding. My Mrs. Right would like some sports and travel.

On the flip side, many men don't often daydream about the emotional connection in their marriage. While they desire it, the nuances are usually abstract. Men typically approach marriage as providers, protectors, and procreators. I use the term "traces" because they might not consciously articulate this desire for everyone. An emotional connection drives a man's longing to fulfill these roles(providers, protectors, and procreators) for their wives. Despite wanting happy and healthy relationships, men, may struggle to articulate their feelings in intricate detail due to their inherent communication style.

On a different note, many men often imagine qualities like "whiplash beauty" and unwavering loyalty in their ideal partners. They desire someone grounded, freed from conventional fantasy expectations, and who prioritizes their faith. This perfect companion supports their hobbies and encourages the exploration of new interests together. In this shared vision, "Welcome home!" is associated with the scent of freshly baked snacks—For some reason a peanut butter cookie is on my mind as I write.

We must temper our expectations and not hold our partners to unrealistic standards based on what we've imagined. Expecting your partner to meet unspoken and unrealistic expectations is not fair to them, and it's not fair to you. Trying to force your partner into a prefabricated mold will not work. Don't prohibit yourself from seeing the best and most unique things about your partner. When you attempt to force them into a prefabricated mold, they fit into your mold, not the authentic beauty within them. Let's get back to the Marriage seed.

Dating with a purpose means prioritizing our life goals and finding a partner who supports them. We all have unique purposes, not just for ourselves but also to help others. Dating purposefully means focusing on our goals and finding a partner who helps us reach them. Having a supportive partner isn't just about achieving things together; it's also about growing as individuals. Living out your calling to love and serve others is more effortless when you're with someone who shares your vision.

Finding a partner who shares your beliefs is crucial to building a solid relationship. When you aren't united in purpose with your partner, you naturally drift apart as your God-ordained paths and purposes differ. The season of purposeful singleness is essential. It allows you the time to discover yourself and helps you find the place or places where you fit. It is in those places and spaces that you will discover your partner.

Biblical courting emphasizes that our desires should take a back seat to our focus on our purpose and mission.

In Genesis, God brought Eve to Adam because He recognized Adam's need for assistance in his mission. Similarly, in Genesis 24, as Abraham sought a wife for his son, Abraham's servant received specific instructions regarding where _not_ to look. This restriction ensured compatibility, as marrying from the servant's homeland might lead to conflicting beliefs. Jesus, too, referred to himself as the bridegroom and us as the bride, emphasizing the importance of aligning our minds for a fruitful spiritual relationship. While our desires hold significance, not all should dictate lifelong commitments. The first biblical mention of marriage occurred when God brought Eve to Adam. Despite recognizing a need, Adam waited for God to provide a suitable option. Don't rush the decision in desperation; keep your eyes open while moving forward.

When you are chasing a common goal together, it only brings you closer to one another.

So, when you're dating with purpose, remember to:

1. **Focus on Goals:** Choose a partner who supports your life goal and whose goals you support.
2. **Share Values:** Look for someone who shares your beliefs and values to avoid conflicts down the road.

3. **Patience:** Don't rush into things; trust that the right person will arrive at the right time.

Considering these points, you can build a robust and lasting relationship.

FOCUS ON GOALS: DATING EXPECTATIONS

Dating begins with the seeds of animated aspirations and expectations. As individuals sort through the seeds in search of one worthy of romantic connections, their minds echo with dreams of the ideal partner—a love story scripted in the stars. Yet, this initial phase is not merely an isolated moment—it is a juncture where expectations converge, setting the stage for the growth of a relationship.

In exploring dating expectations, we dig into societal influences and personal experiences that contribute to the germination of romantic desires. The soil, initially untouched, soon becomes enriched with the nutrients of cultural norms, familial expectations, and the unique imprints of past relationships. The journey of dating expectations is not a solitary planting but a collective emergence of dreams that individuals bring to the shared garden of romantic possibility.

It becomes evident that dating expectations are not arbitrary seeds but reflections of an individual's deepest desires and values. These expectations act as seeds, germinating and growing into the unique plants one envisions for a future partnership. These expectations are the silent hardscape between the present and an envisioned relational future, whether articulated or not.

Dating or courting should never be done in a vacuum. There are so many reasons I say that, but I will only look at two reasons. The first is apparent. Dating costs time and money. I am a very intelligent dater. I am not offensive in any way, but I do not ignore "flags in the play". A relationship includes fun and productivity. As a rule, I am careful of how and where I invest. My budget for fun is much less than my budget for advancement. If there is no hope that the two of us could have a productive future, another meeting would waste a resource. The second reason not to date in a vacuum is that dating is reflective. Reflection means that we look back. It's important to know what you are looking back to and what you are looking back for. I have learned that many reflections were fantasies of what I wanted. I should have looked deeper to see why I wanted what I wanted.

> *A reflection can point to an excellent complement or expose an emotional hurt that requires healing.*

The dichotomy between idealized fantasies and the realities of human connection further compounds the complexities of dating expectations. It is a delicate nurturing process between daydreams often accompanying early infatuation and the tangible, sometimes imperfect, individuals who stand before us. In cultivating dating expectations, we endeavor to decode the unspoken and illuminate the path toward authentic connections grounded in self-awareness and mutual understanding. So, let us till the soil with curiosity and introspection, casting aside preconceived notions and embracing the evolving garden of relational expectations.

Dating unfolds not only in the exchange of words but also in silence.

Silence is a language of unspoken desires.

It is the desire for a partner who understands the nuances of one's unexpressed emotions, the longing for a connection that transcends verbal expression. These unspoken desires act as silent guides, subtly steering individuals toward or away from potential matches.

Understanding the unspoken desires demands unraveling societal conditioning that may suppress authentic expression. It involves peeling back the layers of conformity to reveal the core desires that may not align with conventional expectations. If I spend the rest of my life with someone, I do not want conventional. Maybe it's me, but conventional sounds boring and mundane. How long will that last? Also, if not appropriately navigated, conformity can cause me to lose my authentic self. Indeed, you can conform and maintain your identity, and your partner will have such an understanding of you that they will be able to feed your authentic self, even under the masking of conformity. That hasn't been my story. Therefore, I will expose my longing and desires. The canvas of dating expectations gains depth as these hidden longings come to light, influencing individuals' choices in pursuit of a meaningful connection.

Acknowledging unspoken desires fosters an environment of mutual understanding and acceptance. It requires partners to attune themselves to the silent cues and subtle gestures that communicate volumes beyond spoken words. In doing so, dating transforms into a symphony where each note, though unspoken, resonates with the shared harmony of emotional connection. The shared emotional connection tells the silent communicator that I am known.

This awareness creates an authentic connection based on a mutual understanding of the silent language from the heart.

SHARED VALUES: THE ESSENCE OF EMOTIONAL WELLBEING

Beyond the initial allure and shared interests, compatibility is the root of emotional synchrony, where two hearts create a connection.

Emotional compatibility transcends mere agreement on preferences or alignment in hobbies. It ventures into shared emotional landscapes, establishing a profound connection that withstands the tests of time and circumstance.

When thinking about the reality of life, who talks to you most? The answer is you! Emotions are an interpretation of bodily sensations produced by stimuli within our mind; this is critical because we can't see an emotion. We see or experience the responses formed by the emotion. The response is just a reflex. We may not even know the trustworthy source of the emotions. Like our physical health, we should not settle for treating symptoms. We need to dive deeper and deal with the cause. That is why psychologists suggest that we ask questions about our feelings. Let's dig deeper into our emotional well-being. Let us strengthen our EQ.

At its core, emotional compatibility involves aligning values, aspirations, and responses to life's challenges. The resonance of emotional frequencies allows individuals to navigate the highs and lows of life in tandem, fostering a deep understanding of each other's inner worlds. As partners embark on their journey, exploring emotional compatibility becomes an integral aspect of determining the sustainability of the connection. Discovering whether you and your partner vibe emotionally is like strolling through the various seasons of life and the feelings and responses they bring. Forget the small talk—let's get deep. What makes them tick about happiness, sadness, and all those feelings?

Now, emotional sync-up is like having your secret language. There is no need for fancy words – it's about getting to know each other without saying a thing. It's about having each other's back when times get tough. This part of the book is your guide to spotting if you and your partner are on the same emotional wavelength. Get ready to tune in to those vibes beneath the surface of your chats. It reminds me of a story written about a man named Moses, who knew the ways of the one who loved him, and another group of people who experienced the same things as Moses, but the story says they knew His deeds. Intimacy lies in knowing someone so closely that you can predict what they would do under certain circumstances because you've studied their ways, not just the deeds, which means what they have done. Emotional synchrony helps you know the why, what, and how.

Exploring emotional compatibility serves as a compass for navigating the complexities of dating. It gives individuals insights into whether their emotional worlds align, offering a glimpse into the potential for a lasting connection. As you embark on the dating journey, understanding the essence of emotional synchrony becomes a guiding light, illuminating the path toward meaningful and enduring connections.

SHARED VALUES: THE DYNAMICS OF NURTURING FOR SHARED GROWTH

Within the dating garden, the profound concept of shared growth emerges as a dynamic force, propelling individuals towards a single focal point.

Shared growth extends beyond personal development; it is the collaborative journey of both partners as they navigate the evolving terrain of their relationship. Rather than viewing personal growth as a solitary pursuit, the emphasis shifts towards creating an environment where the relationship catalyzes individual and collective flourishing, growth, and change.

Shared growth involves recognizing that individuals within a relationship are not static entities. Instead, they are evolving beings with the capacity for continuous transformation. This section encourages partners to foster a relational space where each person's growth is acknowledged, interwoven with, and complemented by the development of the other.

Explore practical strategies for nurturing shared growth, emphasizing the importance of open communication about individual goals, aspirations, and areas of personal development. For instance, partners can engage in regular check-ins to discuss their evolving dreams and how they align with the shared vision and mission of the relationship. Active listening and genuine interest in each other's journeys are pivotal in creating a symbiotic relationship where both individuals thrive.

Shared growth also involves navigating challenges collaboratively. Instead of viewing obstacles as hindrances, partners are encouraged to perceive them as opportunities for collective problem-solving and growth. An example could be a couple facing a career-related challenge. Rather than allowing it to create a divide, they can collaboratively explore solutions, supporting each other through the process and strengthening the relationship in the face of adversity.

This type of dynamics can transform the dating experience into a laboratory for resilience. Shared triumphs and navigating adversities become integral to the relationship's narrative.

PATIENCE: GROWING RESILIENCE

Your relationship is fertile ground ready for the growth of seeds. The seeds represent the potential for love, connection, and shared experiences.

Relationships, like the cultivation of seeds, require a nurturing environment. We're not discussing rigid structures but nurturing soil rich in shared values, trust, and open communication. Picture this environment as the fertile ground on which the seeds of your relationship take root. It's the nutrient-rich foundation upon which the bond grows, ensuring stability and endurance.

Similarly, the gardener must till the ground for the best germination from any seed. Plant seeds do not thrive when planted in compacted soil. The ground requires tilling, aerating, or turning for the best result. If the soil is too rigid or compacted, the fragile roots will not be able to receive the nutrients or penetrate the soil to grow.

Trust fortifies healthy relationships, much like the strong roots of a plant. Trust is essential to the relationship, providing stability and nourishment. When partners can depend on each other, the relationship remains strong and resilient, even when facing challenges.

> *Communication is the sunlight that nourishes the growing seeds.*

The ability to express thoughts, feelings, and concerns effectively keeps the relationship well-nurtured to withstand the test of time. Open, honest, and respectful communication is essential for cultivating a solid foundation that connects hearts and minds. Communication is connection. I smile and say thank you, but communication is a skill I have learned. I took classes and went to many coaches, therapists, and mentors who helped me develop my communication skills. As an entrepreneur and a leader, it was my responsibility to communicate goals and objectives, and when I first started, I did all of the training. That's a lot of talking! For me, it never became easy, but it was necessary. The greatest challenge was speaking to a group and communicating the entire message in a manner that everyone would receive and comprehend. The communication nourished the relationships, but it typically drained me. My reward was being understood and benefiting from the results. How much more valuable is communicating with your love than colleagues? I can promise you the rewards are better with a loved one.

Challenges are inevitable in any relationship, like the unpredictable weather affecting growing plants. Like gardeners tending to their plants during storms, couples can embrace challenges as opportunities to strengthen their connection. Anecdotes of real-life couples facing and overcoming adversity become sources of inspiration, encouraging others to patiently nurture their seeds of love and resilience.

CHAPTER 5: FAITH: ACT AS IF IT WILL GROW

Misunderstood things are often seen as negatives when, in reality, they are strengths that deserve recognition. In relationships, it's natural not to see eye to eye on everything, and our faith may take different forms. While clarity in a commitment is crucial, there are many things on our journey to figure out.

Just because something isn't clear doesn't make it wrong. Having a vision means seeing something, but it only guarantees understanding some details within that line of sight. When you operate with faith or a vision, you can see beyond what you and those around you may perceive. Visionaries focus on the long term, not just the present day.

Now, let's talk about faith. In most situations, someone with faith is also a person of strength, and I agree with that assessment. Faith creates an attitude of unwavering resilience. How else can someone see one thing and believe something completely different will come out of it without a logical explanation? Think of the movie Pursuit of Happiness, based on the life of Mr. Chris Gardner, in which Will Smith played the role.

I used to memorize verses from the King James version, and one passage that stood out was Hebrews 11:1. It says, "*Faith is the substance of things hoped for, the evidence of things not seen.*" Another translation says, "*Faith is the confidence that what we hope for will happen; it gives us assurance about things we cannot see.*"

Faith and a vision can be a source of strength and assurance even when things are unclear. Like a visionary, focus on the bigger picture and trust that things will unfold as they should.

People of faith are considered firm and very astute. To be a person of faith, one must endure seasons that do not resemble their expectations. Seasons are different from the happy marriage you have always hoped for, and they are tough. Who wants faith for a happy, healthy, and fulfilling marriage? I don't! Because if I need faith to have that type of marriage, it implies that I don't have one now. Faith, being hope, is required in marriage. We can not see around the corner, so our faith and belief systems guide us successfully through life within our marriage. A happy and healthy marriage is never a perfect union, but the shared principles and expectations strengthen the bonds of happiness in the marriage. Part of the marital bond is knowing that you are not alone, and the ability to lean on each other adds to the fulfillment. Being able to lean on your partner confirms that you made the right decision despite what's happening.

TOLERANCE: THE ART OF ENDURING LOVE

One often overlooked yet profoundly impactful partner for a healthy relationship is tolerance. Let's navigate its complexities by dispelling misconceptions and revealing its transformative power within the covenant of relationships.

Tolerance, often unfairly labeled as a passive compromise, deserves closer examination. It is an active force requiring seeds of self-awareness, strength, and resilience. Maintaining a fair, objective, and permissive attitude is a conscious choice, especially when faced with differing opinions, beliefs, or practices. In relationships, this virtue becomes a dynamic nutrient that begins the germination process of diverse perspectives.

Numerous individuals selfishly lose themselves in the season of faith for health, all because of a seemingly innocuous word – tolerance. Tolerate often has a negative connotation. Yet, by definition, tolerance is neither positive nor negative. Tolerance speaks of the strength or power to endure or accept. You may think highly of yourself, feeling like you've got it all together 24/7. However, in your all-that-self, a season will come – brief or prolonged – when your spouse, yes, yours, will need faith to persevere. During that season, something between both of you will necessitate faith, and it's at this time that the strength of tolerance will keep your bond intact.

Although the word tolerance tends to have negative connotations, it is not harmful. It is a powerful and positive word.

At its core, tolerance is grounded in objective understanding. It doesn't necessitate complete agreement or unqualified support but demands a commitment to fairness. Picture a scenario where partners may hold contrasting views—tolerance steps in as the arbitrator, fostering an environment that accepts and acknowledges differing beliefs without dismissal or devaluing. Dismissing your partner's vantage point can make your partner feel rejected as a person. It's a matter of self-control and strength of will, enabling us to transcend personal biases in pursuit of shared understanding. Even if you disagree, your communication gives you a better understanding of each other, creating a seed of intimacy.

Seasons demanding faith are inevitable in the journey toward a lasting marital union. Tolerance becomes the compass that guides us through these challenging seasons. It acknowledges that there will be moments when faith is required to hold on, and the strength of tolerance acts as an adhesive binding partner. It's an acceptance that does not indicate weakness but rather an opportunity for growth. Tolerance is not merely endurance; it's a proactive force that stems from the choice to accept. It signifies an acknowledgment that, despite disagreements or differences, the relationship is more valuable.

Faith: Act As If It Will Grow

Tolerance creates room for uniqueness, allowing partners to retain their individuality within the shared journey. It's an unspoken agreement that the bond remains even in moments of disagreement.

Faith requires tolerance, and tolerance nurtures faith. The two become interwoven, like the acorn in my yard. When put into action, faith and tolerance will germinate into enduring love. It's an understanding that the complexities of relationships demand a delicate balance, where faith propels us forward, and tolerance ensures the preservation of the connection.

In relationships, tolerance emerges not as a concession but as a virtue. It recognizes that relationships have seasons. Embracing this virtue strengthens the foundation in the face of challenges, echoing a commitment to love that transcends differences.

FAITHFUL STEPS: UNCHARTED TERRITORIES

Relationships often take us into uncharted territories, where uncertainty can obscure the path forward. In these moments, faith emerges as the guiding light, urging partners to take bold and faithful steps into the unknown. Imagine a couple standing at the threshold of commitment, their hearts echoing with the promise of a shared future. Faith becomes the force that propels them forward, transcending fears and uncertainties.

Faith: Act As If It Will Grow

In the Navy, I loved looking out at the horizon from the elevator on the hanger bay at night. It always amazed me to see nothing but stars and the ripples of the water as it broke from the ship's movement. All I saw was water, stars, and the moon. However, deep down inside, although there was no visual evidence, I knew we were on course. How did I know? I had faith in the quartermaster and the navigator. While I didn't know them, I believed they knew the best route for the ship to reach our destination.

Just as sailors navigate the open sea with the guidance of sea navigational calculators, couples navigate the unpredictable seas of love with faith as their compass. Faith becomes the unwavering reference point, offering direction when the journey becomes foggy or tumultuous. It acknowledges that, in the vast expanse of love, having a guiding star is essential to staying the course.

In the symphony of love, planting the seed of trust and openness sets the stage for a beautiful and resilient connection. Just as a seed carefully placed in fertile soil, trust forms the foundation, allowing the roots of a relationship to grow deep. Openness, akin to sunlight, bathes the seed in the warmth of understanding and acceptance.

Faith: Act As If It Will Grow

Planting this seed requires a deliberate act of faith. One must believe that vulnerability is not a weakness but a strength that nurtures the potential for something extraordinary to bloom. As the seed germinates, vulnerability becomes the tender shoot, reaching toward the light of shared dreams and aspirations.

The journey of nurturing this relationship seed is challenging. Like a growing plant facing unexpected weather patterns, couples will encounter obstacles. Expect them. Yet, just as a well-rooted plant withstands storms, the trust and openness in the relationship become a stabilizing force. Whether facing communication differences or external pressures, the shared commitment to the relationship becomes the sturdy stem that supports and guides the flourishing bond.

In this garden of love, partners cultivate a collective strength, each relying on the other's commitment to the shared vision. Planting the seed is an ongoing process that requires continuous care and attention, but with faith, the potential for a thriving and enduring connection is limitless.

Faith: Act As If It Will Grow

Faithful steps involve believing in the potential. It's an unwavering belief that love can evolve and flourish despite the complexities and imperfections. This belief fuels the commitment to weathering storms, knowing that the journey will not always be smooth, but the destination is worth the work.

As partners faithfully take steps into uncharted territories, faithful love unfolds. It creates roots of mutual trust, shared dreams, and the courage to navigate the unknown together. The next journey through a similar storm will not require as much faith as the memory of each joint victory strengthens the roots. Faith becomes a shared language that binds and engages hearts.

Engagement is not a static phase but a journey marked by seasonal shifts. From the exhilarating warmth of shared dreams to the chilly winds of disagreements, couples experience a spectrum of emotions. Tolerance becomes the thermostat that regulates the relationship's temperature, fostering resilience amidst the changing seasons.

The term "tolerance" often carries misconceptions, but it signifies emotional fair play in the context of engagement. It's about maintaining a fair, objective, and permissive attitude toward each other's opinions, beliefs, and practices. In essence, tolerance becomes the bridge that spans the emotional gaps, allowing partners to coexist harmoniously despite differences.

Tolerance develops as a muscle. There were times when I made terrible decisions. While it wasn't necessarily a wrong decision, it could have been bad for now. When you partner with someone, they are affected by your choices. So now, because of the many times my wife had to tolerate me, I became grateful, more appreciative of her, and more tolerant. Why? Because I saw the sacrifices she made for me, I strengthened my understanding of her love for me.

Tolerance is the strength that allows partners to endure these seasons, recognizing that storms do not define the entirety of the relationship. It's the assurance that spring will come despite the winter's chill.

Disagreements are inevitable, and how partners navigate these disagreements defines the depth of their connection. Tolerance manifests as the grace to disagree without dismantling the foundation of love. It's the art of holding opposing views without diminishing the other person's value, fostering an environment where differences are acknowledged and respected.

Compromise is part of relationships, but tolerance brings a different dimension. It's not merely about meeting in the middle but embracing diverse thoughts and perspectives. Tolerance allows partners to coexist without demanding conformity, preserving the individuality that enriches the relationship.

In the face of disagreements or differing viewpoints, tolerance builds bridges rather than walls. It's the recognition that partners can stand on opposite sides of an issue without erecting barriers between them. Tolerance fosters open communication and understanding, ensuring that the fabric of the relationship remains resilient in the face of diverse perspectives.

As partners navigate the engagement seasons, tolerance emerges as the unsung hero, the pillar that upholds the sanctity of lasting love. It's not passive acceptance but an active choice to coexist, learn, and grow together.

I don't know about you, but I would rather have a great and fulfilling marriage than believe in one. I'd rather have faith that the LORD will continue to sustain and prosper and show us how to improve our happy, healthy, and fulfilling marital relationship. For that, there is plenty of work to do!

Both the Word and life teach us that every circumstance has its season. When we find ourselves in a season demanding faith—whether to meet our needs, support our spouse, or brace ourselves—let's maintain an open mind and approach it from a proper vantage point.

I think it is worth repeating that tolerance is a fair, objective, and permissive attitude toward those whose opinions, beliefs, practices, racial or ethnic origins, etc., differ from one's own, freedom from bigotry. Where is the negativity in that definition? I want fair treatment, especially when I know we disagree.

Tolerance means I don't necessarily agree or like the situation and may not support you with it, but I will be objective and not discard you because of it. Tolerance is a matter of self-control and strength of will.

My way sometimes needs to be corrected, and I do not agree with 100% of anything anyone outside of God says. Humanity is not omniscient. Therefore, we will be wrong and experience the wrong done by others. In those moments, faith must kick in so we can endure. That, my friend, requires tolerance and faith in action.

FAITH IN ACTION: THE FOUNDATION OF A PURPOSEFUL UNION

Connection is not just a prelude to marriage; it's a time of deliberate actions that plant the seeds for a purposeful union. In cultivating commitment, partners take on the role of gardeners, carefully tilling their internal grounds and sowing seeds through the choices that will blossom throughout their marital journey.

Intentional Individual Growth

In relationships, couples are not just sowing the seeds of their lives but nurturing two stories, each with unique characters, dreams, and aspirations. Like diligent gardeners, partners recognize the importance of nurturing themselves individually to bring richer narratives to the shared story.

Example: Sarah, an aspiring artist, intentionally cultivates her creativity. She understands that a thriving marriage benefits from her fulfillment within her passions. The joy she feels while exploring her creativity shines through in her partnering.

Shared Values as the Foundation

Shared values become foundational support in their relationship, ensuring stability even in life's complexities. It's not about identical beliefs but finding a rhythm that resonates with both hearts.

Example: James and Maria, through open communication, plant the seeds of their shared values of family, faith, and adventure. These shared values provide a foundation for future understanding and connection within their union.

The Growth of Understanding

Communication is like the nurturing rain of understanding. Partners learn the art of active listening and articulate expression, ensuring their garden reflects mutual comprehension. This intentional communication becomes the heartbeat of the relationship, fostering deep roots.

Example: Mark and Emily establish a communication routine, dedicating time for heartfelt conversations to understand each other's fears, dreams, and expectations.

Financial Planning

Financial problems are one of the top five causes of divorce. Partners aligning their financial goals and values ensure their garden grows in sync regarding budgeting, saving, and future aspirations.

Example: David and Olivia attend financial planning sessions, learning the art of economic collaboration and setting the stage for a secure and well-planned financial future.

Balancing Independence and Togetherness

The balancing act between independence and togetherness is unique to the individuals within each relationship. Partners recognize the importance of maintaining individual identities while nurturing a shared life. The garden involves respecting personal space, cultivating individual hobbies, and celebrating the beauty of unity within diversity.

Example: Chris and Jessica, recognizing their need for shared moments and personal pursuits, cultivate a balance that enriches their engagement garden.

As a Christian, my faith hinges on tolerance, holding on to what I believe, even when I can't see it. Romans 11:18-32 shows us a clear picture of the strength required for toleration. The passage identifies the diversity of ways the Father has revealed Himself to us. It takes love to accept what you do not like and live in an environment with opposition. It's even more complicated when the willful opposition is from the one you love. Toleration says, "I am not going anywhere because I know it will improve." That is not negative; it is positive.

The issue arises when we entrust feelings rather than faith and reason with the responsibility of navigating these intense and pivotal seasons. Feelings are, by nature, internal and self-seeking. They operate in isolation and fail to consider external facts. While I may not desire to feel tolerated, these feelings exist. My spouse and I worked through this challenging season even when we disagreed.

UNDERSTANDING FAITH IN RELATIONSHIPS

Acting in faith is challenging, but it is so important in relationships. Beyond religious doctrines, faith in relationships propels us into the unknown, urging us to believe in the unseen and positively navigate uncharted territories.

All relationships face a paradox: We must believe in the potential of something we cannot fully perceive. Faith bridges what we know and what is yet to unfold. It's not merely an abstract concept but a tangible force that allows us to invest in our partners' unseen qualities, virtues, and potential. Just as in the movie Pursuit of Happiness, where the leading character holds on to his vision despite the stark realities, relationships require a similar steadfast belief in a future that transcends current circumstances.

While vision is often associated with clarity, it only provides a partial roadmap. Relationships demand a visionary focus, not just on the present but on a distant horizon where growth, challenges, and shared triumphs await. The concept of a 'journey' comes alive here – a journey that requires faith in the unseen chapters of our relationship.

Faith in relationships is not passive; it's a dynamic force that calls for action. It prompts us to move beyond mere comprehension, encouraging a proactive belief in the potential of our unions. It's an acknowledgment that, even without total clarity, our steps move toward a purpose. This active faith transforms relationships from static agreements to living, breathing entities that evolve with each shared step. Faith may only sometimes provide immediate clarity, but it doesn't negate its significance. Clarity is crucial, but it often unfolds gradually, akin to the germination of a plant. The interplay between faith and clarity propels relationships forward, complementing the other. Understanding that not having all the answers doesn't diminish the journey's strength but adds an element of mystery and excitement. If nothing else, unclarity allows partners to communicate and share their feelings about where they are and the path that they are on. Faith in relationships can create a solid bond.

Faith becomes a silent ally in achieving shared goals. It aligns our aspirations with an overarching purpose and a flourishing partnership.

As we navigate the covenant of engagement, let's embrace the profound reality that relationships are, at their core, a testament to faith. The binding force transcends the visible, transforming unions into a journey of shared beliefs, aspirations, and a future written in the ink of mutual trust.

Marriage is fundamentally a journey of faith. Like a seed with a protective shell, we remain unaware of what is within. Exposing our essence brings forth a range of emotions, physical challenges, and spiritual revelations. Just as faith is necessary to love and please God, who is love, it is also essential to love our spouses. We won't comprehend everything, and that's okay because constant self-discovery is part of the journey.

Tolerance alone isn't enough to accommodate your spouse's unique qualities and doesn't create a real sense of love. You must give and receive faith, understanding, and forgiveness to have love. Love is like a river that keeps going, covering, accepting, and giving. It should always be there in our lives.

How can two people walk together unless they agree? They can't! Mutual agreement on directions, pace, and timing is essential for walking together. Distinct from destiny, direction outlines the route leading to the intended destiny. It is crucial to agree on this path for a harmonious journey.

Once you agree on the trajectory you desire for your relationship, the pace becomes the next point of agreement. Travel speed is determined by considering terrain, fatigue, and environmental conditions, ensuring a smooth journey.

The direction and pace you want to travel in your relationship must be accepted and applied by both partners to reach the destination on time. Any discord on these aspects can impede progress toward the shared destiny. This challenge resonates from personal experiences in my marriage. My ex-wife and I expressed our desire for a better quality of life. Conversations about dreams and plans were abundant, but the stumbling block wasn't in hearing but in listening.

Let's talk about what it means to be a good listener in a relationship. Hearing is just picking up sound, but truly listening to another person is a whole other level. It's about understanding and responding, not just to the words but also to the feelings behind them. For example, when you read a text, you miss out on the tone and body language that add depth to communication. You need to look for and understand those things as a good listener in a relationship.

In relationships, being a good listener goes beyond hearing the words someone says. It's about paying attention to the emotions and feelings they're trying to express. I've been there—I listened to the words but didn't understand what my partner felt. It happens when we're not fully tuned in.

A good listener is crucial, especially when your partner shares something important. If you're not paying attention, it can make them feel like you're not there for them. Imagine your partner opening up about something personal—just hearing the words isn't enough. You must genuinely listen to understand their emotions and show that you care. Otherwise, communication will break down, and your partner will feel unheard, uncared for, and likely upset.

If you neglect this part of listening, it can harm your relationship. Your partner may feel that you need to give them the attention and understanding they need. When this happens, you miss out on connecting at a deeper level. In a healthy relationship, being a good listener creates trust, intimacy, and a firm foundation that stands the test of time.

Here are ten practical tips for being a good listener:

1. **Give Your Full Attention:** When someone is talking to you, put away distractions like your phone or TV and focus on what they're saying.

2. **Make Eye Contact:** Look at the person speaking. It shows them that you are engaged and listening.

3. **Don't Interrupt:** Let the person finish talking before you respond. It helps them feel heard.

4. **Show You're Listening:** Nod your head or use other non-verbal cues to show you are paying attention.

5. **Ask Questions:** If you need clarification, ask questions. Asking questions positions you to receive understanding and shows that you are interested.

6. **Repeat Back:** Repeat a summary of what the person said to ensure you understood correctly. It shows you are actively listening.

7. **Empathize:** Try to understand the person's feelings and point of view. Show that you care about what they're going through.

8. **Avoid Judging:** Keep an open mind. Try not to judge or criticize what the person is sharing with you.

9. **Be Patient:** Sometimes, people need time to express themselves. Be patient and let them take their time.

10. **Stay Calm:** Even if the conversation gets emotional, try to stay calm. Staying calm will help create a safe space for open communication.

So, being a good listener means more than hearing words; it's about understanding emotions, empathizing, and responding with care. This skill strengthens your relationship, making it a safe and supportive space where you feel genuinely heard and valued.

CHAPTER 6:
GERMINATION - IN THE BEGINNING

For a relationship to grow, you must be open to change and learn to grow with each other. Pastor Ron Carpenter talks about relationships being like seeds—they have the potential to develop into something more. This lesson is about using that idea to improve relationships and marriages.

There is a connection between your purpose, the reason for your creation, and who you are married to. Initially, the marriage plan was about giving and working together. In the Garden of Eden, Adam was responsible for caring for things, which meant he had to be attentive and work on them. He needed to watch and tend to them, showing they required attention and awareness.

Germination - In the Beginning

It's interesting to consider God's role in this. God saw that Adam shouldn't be alone, so He promised to make a helper for him. But then, God started making animals. It seems like God had a plan. Placing Adam in a garden was intentional. God recognized Adam's need and set things in motion.

The law of the harvest is simple: You plant a seed, wait, and then you get the result. In this case, Adam's need is the seed, the time is the waiting and working period, and the harvest is Eve—someone who complements him and is the result of his work and waiting.

We learned from the Garden of Eden experience that before you find your Eve (or Boaz), you must know who you are and to whom you belong. A clear picture was painted in the Garden of Adam, maintaining order and doing the required work, totally submitting to God. That is easy, but is it? God made Adam, noticed a need (void), and expected Adam to function well with the need. So, real questions to discover authenticity include: How do you handle pressure? Can you function with a need without everyone around you noticing? Do you get upset because of the void? Can you have a need and still see that what's walking in front of you is not suitable?

In marriage, your priorities change. Your spouse becomes the main focus, even more important than your family, friends, or spiritual purpose. Before marriage, you must ensure your partner aligns with your life's purpose.

When it comes to dating and courting, authenticity is crucial. The main question is understanding yourself—who you are and what you stand for. The Garden of Eden story teaches us that you must know and be true to yourself before finding the right partner. Understanding how you handle pressure, dealing with needs, and noticing what suits you is also essential.

While people can help along the way, a connection with something bigger, like God, can uniquely fulfill needs. There's no strict rule that God has one specific person for you to marry. It's more about aligning with your destiny than following a predetermined plan. As you explore relationships, keep true to yourself. We often get so caught up in finding our mate that we either lower our standards or become so in love with marriage that we let our guard down before we know if the person we are with is safe.

I recall my courting experience. I often began to like the person I was with so much that I would justify their actions.

Germination - In the Beginning

Don't get me wrong, there is nothing wrong with being gracious, but if you are going to justify character flaws, find the source. You need to know the seed planted in their life that brought forth the fruit to know if justification is appropriate or if they need help. The desire to be in a relationship can affect our discernment. While forgiving is liberating, justifying behaviors or compromising your standards is not a good practice for both parties.

As a partner, sometimes seeking the best for someone involves forgiveness, taking action, and recommending they seek help. The marital covenant provides a safe place to reside and become the best version of themselves. I vividly recall our first date; she probably thought I was crazy. Yet, amidst the laughter, smiles, and people-watching, there was a shift. My gaming face came on, and I began revealing some of the challenges I had faced in life. While I didn't completely understand myself then, I knew the aspects that bothered me. I recognized the importance of connecting with someone who might have concerns about my past – rightfully so – but was more focused on where I was at that moment and where I was heading.

There's one phrase she probably never wants to hear again, my "this will surely make her run" statement:

"Everyone has a crazy; I just need to make sure your crazy won't kill me, and you need to make sure mine won't kill you." It may sound peculiar, but I meant that if we are contemplating entering into a marital covenant, let's do it with complete transparency. Let's lay everything on the table to make an informed and sound decision.

At the age of 4o and beyond, both of us had a clear understanding of what we didn't want or like. I preferred to provide reasons to keep the shell hard. My objective was to assist her in maintaining that tough exterior so she could make a well-informed decision. However, I knew it wouldn't be easy because our outer shell would ultimately break. The idea of being broken isn't something anyone eagerly anticipates.

Comparing our journey to a flower shop, you might see a picture of an arrangement when you're seeking flowers. However, the contents inside that package and the image on the package are different. What you can hold in your hands might appear brown or white, oddly shaped, and far from beautiful. The true beauty of a flower arrangement emerges when planted in soil; nurturing and care occur over time.

Germination - In the Beginning

Like a skilled florist who understands the various flower varieties available each season, our marriage requires intentional care. The florist considers factors like sunlight needs, water requirements, and the time it takes for stems to wither if cut. Each flower's unique characteristics, including the placement of buds on the stalk, are considered when arranging them. After these considerations, the florist relies on their sight to ensure an inviting color scheme and complimentary scents, resulting in a beautiful arrangement. Likewise, our marriage demands intentional efforts to water, feed, and fertilize, ensuring its continuous growth and beauty.

Here are nine tips for your relationship journey:

1. **Be Open to Change:** Just like a seed grows into a plant, relationships have the potential to grow. Be open to change and learn from each other. Embrace the idea that both of you can evolve and develop over time.

2. **Prioritize Your Spouse:** Your partner becomes the main focus in marriage. Ensure your priorities align and your partner supports your life's purpose. Prioritizing your spouse means adjusting your

focus from family, friends, or other aspects of life to your spouse.

3. **Authenticity in Dating:** Before finding the right partner, it's crucial to understand and be true to yourself. Reflect on handling pressure, dealing with needs, and recognizing what suits you. Authenticity is critical in building a solid foundation for a relationship.

4. **Maintain Your Standards:** Don't let the desire for a relationship compromise your standards. While forgiveness is essential, justifying behaviors or lowering your standards is not a good practice. Understand the source of character flaws and be discerning.

5. **Encourage Growth:** As partners, support each other in becoming the best versions of yourselves. Becoming your best version involves forgiveness, action, or the recommendation to seek help. The marital covenant aids personal growth and development.

6. **Transparency in Relationships:** Approach relationships with openness. Share everything to

make informed decisions. Discuss challenges, past experiences, and future goals openly. Transparency is vital for building trust and understanding.

7. **Learn from Past Experiences:** Reflect on past experiences and learnings. Understand what you want and don't want in a relationship. Use this knowledge to guide your decisions and contribute to the relationship's growth.

8. **Embrace Growth as a Process:** Like a flower growing in a garden, recognize that personal and relational growth is a process. Be patient, nurture the relationship, and provide intentional care. Understand that, like flowers, true beauty emerges over time with nurturing and effort.

9. **Intentional Efforts for Growth:** Treat your marriage like a skilled florist treats flowers. Put intentional efforts into watering, feeding, and fertilizing the relationship. Consider each other's unique characteristics and work together to create a beautiful and thriving arrangement.

Applying these practical tips can help you create a relationship that grows and evolves and becomes a source of mutual support and fulfillment.

CHAPTER 7: THE BIG COVER-UP

We all have imperfections; it's just part of being human. So, why are we surprised when we find out someone has made a mistake? This idea comes from being made of dirt; like dirt, we can leave a mark when touched. It's not shocking if you think about it. We all inherited flaws from our ancestors—Adam in the Garden. Even if we try to start fresh with a new outlook, we must abandon the old habits.

Knowing this, both partners in a marriage have their quirks. The important thing is to acknowledge this reality; as Bill Hybel mentions in his book "Honest to God," being truthful starts with being honest with ourselves and God before being open with others. In marriages, honesty is a big deal, but often, people focus only on being honest about what they hear from others. However, how we see ourselves has a more significant impact on a marriage than what others tell us. The truth we get is always influenced by how the person sharing it sees things.

My studies and self-introspection taught me that honesty is relative. Perspectives on honesty vary based on personal experiences and interpretations.

The truth most people miss is the truth of themselves. Have you ever met someone and asked yourself, "Why are they wearing that?" Or perhaps you know someone who has no idea that they shoot flaming swords with their tongue? If you were to tell that individual about their actions, they would probably be in denial and suggest that you are embellishing a little. Until we can accept ourselves and our quirks, we will not have a good perception of life or others. When your internal lenses are dirty, nothing you see will be clear.

Discovering ourselves and our quirks isn't just about becoming aware and making excuses; it's about identifying areas in our lives that need tweaking for improvement. We must reach a point where we can be honest with ourselves without harboring hatred or disliking who we are. Only when we acknowledge an issue can we truly address it.

The Big Cover-up

I recall a conversation with my wife about relationships. Everyone wants to find one person to love them for them, yet so many people do not love themselves, and even more don't honestly know themselves. The problem lies in the cover-up. You meet someone who falls in love with your representative. Then it happens. The real you shows up. When that happens, without honesty and effort to work through it, your partner may struggle because the person they see now isn't the one they committed to in the covenant. However, by acknowledging this honestly, we can address it together and grow stronger.

We need courage and strength to live unashamedly. We are made from dirt and born in sin, so why are we so surprised when we see dirt on others? It may be time to clean your mirror.

I truly understand the sentiment of learning the difference between your partner and your partner's representative. It's an unraveling, discouraging, and heartbreaking experience. Yet, in this fallen world that prioritizes self-interest, promoting the idea of "getting mine" or the old favorite "do you boo," why are we surprised? In many instances, the pain, hurt, and disappointment we endure in relationships directly result from someone prioritizing their desires. The issue lies in the lack of emphasis on the "US" factor. We don't exist in a vacuum. As we learned in elementary science, there is a reaction to every action. This principle holds in relationships as well.

Sayings like "Do you" or "Get yours" can be acceptable in some contexts but are never adequate in a relationship. I'm not saying we should lose our identity. Never do that. The differences in our creation allow us to be more complimentary. Yes, you guessed it, my viewpoint is that of a complementation. The purpose of Adam's creation was to further the creation process by caring for what God created. Eve's purpose was to help in that task. It was their complimenting differences that brought Adam joy! God's design was flawless. A suitable help! Eve helped Adam in ways that no other could. It was a match made from heaven!

Now, let's reflect on the day and the way they met. First, Adam was doing something. Maybe he was working the dirt, chasing or naming animals, or learning to swing from a tree like Tarzan. I don't know. I know that when Eve crossed his path, he stopped because what he saw was good!

Now, let's figure out what Eve was doing. Since God presented her to Adam, we know she was submitted and committed to following the Lord's instructions. The scriptures do not mention Eve speaking a word at their initial meeting, so her character and beauty spoke for her.

Now, let's briefly examine Adam and Eve. They were both naked, and neither was ashamed. Relational nakedness is equivalent to transparency.

> *Being fully transparent in marriage builds trust, deepens emotional intimacy, and fosters a stronger connection between partners.*

It allows both individuals to address challenges openly, preventing misunderstandings and creating a safe space for growth. Transparency and acceptance lay the foundation for a healthy, resilient relationship where both partners feel seen, valued, and supported. Transparency and unconditional acceptance are the missing ingredients in many relationships.

> *Transparency and acceptance produce trust and security.*

Transparency and acceptance produce trust and security. The Garden was home to Adam and Eve, where they could enjoy each other authentically.

Building a nest, creating a home—these phrases evoke a sense of warmth, stability, and shared experience. As we navigate the intricacies of relationships, particularly marriages, it becomes evident that constructing a home extends beyond the physical realm of bricks and mortar; it involves crafting a sanctuary for emotions, understanding, and love to flourish.

Love, the cornerstone of every marriage, is an intentional force that demands our active engagement.

> *Love is not a feeling but rather a choice.*

The journey from courtship to the shared spaces of marriage is a transition that often alters the dynamics of love. The initial enthusiasm for dating will wane as daily routines, responsibilities, and familiarity set in. Where routine sets in, intentionality becomes paramount. Adam and Eve can thrive forever if they keep the uniqueness discovered when they met in the equation at all times. Adam wasn't alone in the garden, but there was none like Eve!!

In the early stages of courtship, the plant is self-sustaining, flourishing effortlessly. However, once familiarity sets in, it requires deliberate care and attention. Neglect can lead to withering, and relationships, like plants, need nourishment to thrive. The watering can of intentionality is what keeps the roots of your relationship positioned to receive the nutrients in the soil.

It's in the gentle touch, thoughtful gesture, expression of gratitude, and willingness to listen. When done deliberately, these small acts create an atmosphere where love can breathe and grow. As the saying goes, "Love is not just something you feel; it's something you do."

Honor, the other twin of this intentional duo, uniquely complements love. To honor your partner is to regard them with great respect and admiration. It involves recognizing and appreciating their intrinsic value and understanding that they bring something unique to the relationship—and, more importantly, to you! In this relational journey, honor is the compass that guides us through the complexities of shared living.

Honor, however, is not a one-time ceremony but an ongoing practice. It's the continuous acknowledgment of your partner's worth, even in moments of disagreement or challenge. Consider the beauty of a garden; it thrives when each flower is honored for its uniqueness. Similarly, recognizing and honoring your partner's individuality in a marriage creates an environment where both can blossom.

The reciprocity of love and honor is a dynamic interaction that requires synchronization. It's a continuous give-and-take, an ebb-and-flow where each partner contributes to the rhythm of the relationship. Expecting love and honor without offering them in return is akin to hoping for a harvest without sowing seeds. The intentionality of one sets the stage for the expectation of the other.

Often, marriage struggles arise when partners fail to understand the changing landscape and fail to honor. What was effortless in the dating phase requires conscious effort in the shared marriage space.

> *Transitioning from "making yourself at home" to "making a home together" is crucial.*

When dating, visiting, and spending time together feels like an adventure, a voluntary choice. In contrast, living together introduces the dynamics of daily life, where choices become intertwined and mutual submission becomes an essential aspect of creating a home. It's a shift from the spontaneity of dating to sharing responsibilities.

Mutual submission, an often-misunderstood concept, is not about dominance or subservience. It's the intentional act of considering, respecting, and honoring each other's needs, perspectives, and aspirations. The shell of individuality cracks, allowing the seed of shared dreams, goals, and a home to germinate and flourish.

Making a home is more than just a physical space; it encompasses the emotional and spiritual dimensions of shared living. It creates an environment where both partners feel seen, heard, and valued. Each of those feelings should be more significant at home than anywhere else! Feelings of acceptance, love, and support fill a home's atmosphere.

Consider the image of a bird meticulously building a nest. With care and purpose, the bird places each twig and strand of grass. The nest is not just a structure; it's a haven, a place of safety and nurture. Similarly, building a home involves carefully selecting words and actions and providing emotional security in a marriage.

Creating a home together requires vulnerability and openness. It's about being naked and unashamedly authentic, allowing one's true self to be seen and accepted. This vulnerability is the key to genuine intimacy, where partners can genuinely care for each other without the weight of concealment. It's a commitment to living naked and unashamed, acknowledging imperfections, and embracing the growth journey together.

The intentional twins, love and honor, guide the hands that lay the foundation and build the home's walls. They are the architects of a sanctuary where the seeds of dreams, aspirations, and a lasting partnership take root.

Intentionality becomes the gardener's tool in the garden of marriage. It's the careful tending to the emotional soil, removing weeds of misunderstanding, and constantly watering love and honor. The seasons of marriage may bring storms and sunshine, but the intentional gardener knows how to navigate each season, ensuring the garden continues to bloom.

So, as you navigate the journey, let love and honor be the guiding forces shaping your relationship. Deliberately cultivate the soil of your relationship and watch as the seeds you plant today blossom into shared memories, dreams, and enduring love.

May your home be a testament to your intentional choices, a haven where love and honor intertwine to create a masterpiece of a shared life.

Yes, a relationship has much more liberty when free and not part of a big cover-up.

> *Keep love and honor in everything that you do.*

Don't get me wrong, living uncovered is scary at times! We do not know how others will take our nakedness. You don't know; revelation takes place during the journey of discovery. We all have a fear of rejection. That is natural. We all struggle with a thing called pride. Fear of rejection is an emotional struggle. And so is pride. The only way to overcome them is to face them head-on. Declaring to ourselves, "No more cover-ups!" And leaning on the LORD to lead us to a place where we can remove the weight of cover-up and be naked.

That is where true intimacy begins. How can you know if someone genuinely cares for you if you are hiding? Have you ever just wanted someone to love you for you? Can someone accurately accuse you of not loving them if you have never seen an authentic person?

Before our emotions take us on a lonely journey and we think they don't care, we ask, "Who have I presented them to love?" Could it be that they can't love you because they never saw you? Could the hard shell on the seed deflect the love intended for you? Have you asked the second question? Can they see me? Most people today struggle with their own identity; therefore, it is difficult for them to be naked, with no shame, and not hide themself. Some are not by choice because they don't even know themselves.

So, when we think of being naked and not ashamed, we need to assess ourselves first honestly. How can I be naked before others when I'm ashamed of my nakedness? Please know I am not condoning the actions that dirt does, but we should face it and acknowledge it. That is the true beauty of salvation: It is liberating. When we get to a place where we refuse to allow our pride to continue to go unchecked and in denial, we accept that we need help! We are not self-made anything. There is someone more significant. It is not until we learn that truth that we can acknowledge our flaws to begin living in nakedness without shame. After all, we are unique beings, flaws and all!

Recognize that differences in opinion, hobbies, or approaches to life can enhance the richness of our relationships. Rather than seeing differences as obstacles, view them as opportunities for growth and enrichment. Covering up our flaws stunts our growth. Regarding relationship enrichment and enhancement, I'd say "Be you" and "Do you" are appropriate because being and doing what comes naturally is in the context of our relationship. We consider the choice we made to love.

Cultivating mutual respect is an ongoing process in the garden of marriage that requires attention, care, and dedication. As partners actively nurture this foundation, they lay the groundwork for a relationship that survives and thrives, blossoming into a beautiful sharing of experiences. That's what we want.

After we have accepted our nakedness and the shame is gone, representing ourselves to God, our creator, puts us in the perfect place to learn our identity. He will lead us to the place we are supposed to be. Now, I understand that everyone who reads this book believes as I believe. That is okay; the truth is, I wrote this book for everyone, but my reflections are based not only on my studies but also on my vantage point, which includes that of someone greater than me. If you don't believe there is a God, I'm sure you have intuition and gut feelings, or maybe it is simply fleeting thoughts. For this writing, it's not important what you call him or it; instead, you listen to your internal compass however you define it.

Was that too spiritual? Let me state this: Do you remember the coincidental elimination of the job you wanted and being overlooked for another? That was His leading. Do you remember when you couldn't find your keys right before work, and you rode past an accident on the side of the road? That is divine orchestration. When you have a hunch, should you circle the parking lot again and find a better parking spot? Divinely orchestrated. What about that silence when you see someone you can't stand approaching? You had all planned what you were going to say and what you were going to do, despite that soft internal voice telling you the wrong. Ready to verbally blast, all that came out of your mouth was "Good morning." He was leading.

God's leading doesn't necessarily make us do right or the situation right. Still, it shows our nakedness and imperfections so we can be more grateful to God, levelheaded with ourselves, and understanding of others.

CHAPTER 8: ACTIVE BLOOMS

Relationships can be challenging and filled with ups and downs. It's normal for people to talk about the challenges and emotions of it. Just like life has different seasons, relationships have them, too. The important part is that we can create a positive atmosphere, especially one filled with love.

Life throws curveballs at everyone, but how we react is up to us. Addressing the proverbial curveballs is crucial in relationships. The critical question is: Are we actively trying to bring happiness and peace into our relationships? It's not about waiting for good things to happen; it's about making them happen.

Think of it like taking care of a garden. You don't expect flowers to bloom independently; you must put in effort and attention. Similarly, creating joy and peace in a relationship requires intentional actions and decisions.

If you are not working towards happiness in your relationship, it's time to ask why. How can you expect joy and peace if you're not actively trying to bring them in? Our actions shape the emotional atmosphere of our relationships.

So, ask yourself: What are you doing on purpose to bring joy and peace into your marriage? This question reminds us that we can shape happiness and harmony in our relationships by actively participating in their ongoing creation.

No matter your faith, let's agree that all marriages should have at least two characteristics: love and honor. I call them the intentional twins because both require intentionality. Showing love and honor requires us to actively participate in ensuring its success. Let's look at each one separately, as they are both verbs, which implies action!

Can an action take place without your participation? The answer is no! Then how do you expect your relationship to improve if you don't do something? It's all up to you!

At the altar, courthouse, beach, while free-falling from a plane, wherever you made your vows, chances are, both of you committed to "do right by" despite the other or whatever life brings.

Being grateful for a loving and caring spouse is a cornerstone of a fulfilling relationship. However, what if the love and honor you expected from your spouse are less palpable than you thought? If your spouse committed to be with you and desired to love and honor you while dating and during the courtship, then your expectation is not as apparent to them. Remember what we said: love and honor are the intentional twins. It requires effort to communicate the need and not just assume. Once spoken, your partner has the wherewithal to actively and intentionally meet the expectations and needs. Now, if your partner is aware of the need and doesn't try to meet that need, that action becomes an intentional withholding. What if, instead of intentional withholding, it stems from a genuine struggle to express these emotions?

In understanding human behavior, it's essential to recognize that individuals often act based on what they are familiar with. There is a natural inclination to conceal weaknesses as a self-protective mechanism. While this doesn't justify certain behaviors, it invites a nuanced perspective – urging us not to hastily judge the observed symptoms without delving into the root causes.

Consider this: the apparent "issue" might manifest deeper feelings of inadequacy within your loved one. Behavioral issues are not an excuse for hurtful actions but rather an invitation to approach the situation with empathy and a willingness to understand the underlying emotions. Relationship dynamics change when you live together. Ask yourself, "Has there been a shift in how expressions of love and honor manifest since our relationship started?"

It's worth contemplating that seeing love and respect is often more straightforward during the dating phase than in the complexities of married life. A lack of intentionality is often the cause of our partners needing the emotional nutrients that make them feel accepted. Intentionality is the conscious effort to express affection and respect that tends to wane as the comfort of shared living sets in. Intentionally expressing love helps replenish your partner's emotional bank. If you are like me, many fleeting thoughts flow through your mind. Learning to share those thoughts removes the need for some creative dialog. It operates like a natural spring from your heart and mind, flowing directly to your partner's ears, mind, and heart, as a natural spring waters its environment. Just lift the dam on your emotions that already exist. Sharing your heart waters the seed of acceptance, love, and honor within your partner.

Both parties in a relationship are responsible for effective communication. Have you watered your partner's seed by sharing your thoughts? Did you know that the words you speak to your spouse can bring life and joy to them? If you answered no, then instead of nurturing the relationship, the lack of intentional effort on all sides of communication can breed insecurity. It is crucial to consider the possibility that your loved one's actions are a way of dealing with their insecurities rather than quickly jumping to conclusions. This realization calls for a pause in judgment and an embrace of understanding.

It also presents an opportunity to reintroduce intentionality into the relationship. Actively and purposefully demonstrating love and honor becomes not only a key to overcoming challenges but also a means of fostering a thriving and fulfilling partnership. The intentional effort to rekindle the spark that characterized the dating phase becomes instrumental in maintaining a positive emotional climate within the marriage.

Divorcenet.com published an article outlining the top 20 Secrets to A Great Marriage,[1] And each step revealed the need to be intentional. What other relationship do you have that you expect to prosper and excel without putting effort into? The simple things we do while dating only cross our subliminal mind, which we must harness. If I don't intentionally travel to see you, I won't see you. If we don't live together when we see each other, a certain level of honor and love expressed unintentionally can subtly change when you get married and share the duplicate house keys and bed. While dating, even when you visit one another, you make yourself at home, but there is a level of servitude that comes automatically with hosting. Likewise, there is gratitude that you are allowed to make yourself at home. Making yourself at home implies you're not home.

---

[1] Lina Guillen, A. (UC L. S. F. (2018, September 11). *Top 20 Secrets to Building a Great Marriage*. www.divorcenet.com.
http://www.divorcenet.com/states/nationwide/secrets_for_great_marriage#

Mutual submission, honor, and gratitude in a relationship aren't just for the early days of living together; they're ongoing, especially when building a home. Think of it like a seed—to grow well, it needs a protective shell to crack open. Similarly, in a relationship, it's when we learn to submit to each other that things can blossom positively.

Mutual submission means both partners work together to create a space where they can thrive. It's not about giving up control but understanding each other's needs and ensuring both people feel supported. Mutual submission allows both partners to contribute to the relationship's well-being.

Honor and gratitude are necessary components of your relationship. Honoring each other means recognizing and celebrating each other's strengths and efforts. Gratitude is about being thankful for the shared journey and appreciating what each person brings to the relationship.

Imagine the relationship as a seed that needs the right environment to grow. Mutual submission, honor, and gratitude create a healthy environment. It's not about being weak but showing strength through humility, understanding, and a commitment to each other.

I want to offer some food for thought, and of course, I will use my life as an example.

No good parent has a problem with submission. Here are a few questions: do you always want to attend your children's events? Don't judge me; sometimes I am tired from work and other responsibilities, but I submit. It is not just me paying for those darn uniforms; they are expensive! Nor the fact that I spent so much time playing Uber Dad for practices that I want to see them perform. There was a time when I lived in southern New Jersey and worked in New York. I had a two-hour commute each way and would be at most of the kid's track practices. Despite my fatigue, I submitted my desire to rest to get under the mission of being a present and active dad. I'm sure the coaches were grateful. Am I the only person who has ever struggled to drive the speed limit when no one is around? Who would know? What's an extra five to ten miles per hour? After all, I am swamped and could use the extra time. Yet, if stopped for speeding, most of us would never say, "It was only ten miles over the speed limit?" I learned to submit to either the ticket or slow down.

> *Submission is simply taking everything into account and actively considering another.*

So, the journey from making yourself at home to making a home is an ongoing process of working together, respecting each other, and appreciating your journey together. It's like cracking open the protective shell to let the relationship grow into something vibrant and lasting.

Let's dig a little deeper to learn what honor is all about. It's an important concept to comprehend fully. Sometimes, we may not take the word as seriously as we should. Perhaps it conjures up imagery from samurai movies and seems irrelevant to your life today. However, honor is a concept that is critically important to all relationships.

Honor means to regard with great respect, which means admiring deeply. Honor forces you to focus on the positive. It doesn't matter what you're feeling now; what about your "co-seed" makes you want to live together?

Honor and respect are closely related concepts essential to building strong and healthy relationships.

> *Honor forces us to focus on the positive, to recognize the good in others, and to treat them with the respect and admiration they deserve.*

It doesn't matter what we're feeling now; what is essential is what we see in our "co-seed" that makes us want to live together. Let us focus on our shared values and goals and work together to achieve them. Respect, founded on deep admiration, prompts us to recognize and appreciate the commendable qualities that define a person.

The notion of honor encourages introspection into our relationships, prompting us to ponder what it is about our "co-seed" – a term symbolizing shared essence and growth potential – that inspires a commitment to navigate life together. This contemplation necessitates concentrating on shared values, collective objectives, and the harmonious fusion of aspirations that lay the groundwork for a shared life.

The pursuit of honor prompts a continuous process of acknowledging and celebrating the positive aspects of our relationships. I used "pursuit" because honoring others doesn't come naturally. Honor may not be natural, but it is necessary. It encourages cultivating an environment where individuals feel acknowledged, valued, and comprehended. This intentional focus on positivity elevates the quality of our connections and contributes to the overall well-being of those involved.

Here are some practical tips on how to show honor in a relationship:

1. **Listen Actively:** Give them your full attention when the other person is talking. Put away distractions and show that what they say is essential to you. Simply put, be present in the moment.

2. **Respect Their Opinions:** Even if you disagree, respect their right to opinions. Avoid belittling or dismissing their views. One of the greatest gifts in a relationship is having another vantage point. It provides an opportunity to learn and grow.

3. **Express Gratitude:** Regularly acknowledge and appreciate the positive things they bring to the relationship. Expressing gratitude fosters a sense of honor and keeps our partners' values in mind. It's hard to fall into the trap of underappreciation in a

relationship when gratitude is in your head and heart.

4. **Use Polite Language:** Be mindful of your words and choose polite and respectful language. Communicating with polite language includes avoiding sarcasm or hurtful comments. Enough said. I will drop the proverbial microphone here.

5. **Be Reliable:** Honor commitments and be someone they can rely on. When you are in a relationship with a reliable person, not only does it build trust, but reliability also shows that you value their time and trust.

6. **Apologize When Necessary:** If you make a mistake, apologize sincerely. Taking responsibility for your actions demonstrates respect for the other person.

7. **Value Their Time:** Be punctual and respect their time. Showing up on time and being considerate of their schedule demonstrates honor. Time is an irreplaceable asset. Value them by never taking something offered that you can never repay.

8. **Encourage Their Goals:** Support and encourage their aspirations and goals. Be a source of motivation rather than a hindrance.

9. **Celebrate Achievements:** Acknowledge and celebrate their successes, big or small. Celebrating achievement shows that you take pride in their accomplishments.

10. **Give Them Personal Space:** Recognize and respect their need for personal space and time alone. Everyone needs moments of solitude.

11. **Be Thoughtful.** Show honor through small gestures of thoughtfulness, like remembering essential dates or surprising them with a just-because gift.

12. **Avoid Public Criticism:** Refrain from publicly criticizing or embarrassing them. Address concerns privately to maintain their dignity.

13. **Practice Empathy.** Put yourself in your partner's shoes and try to understand their perspective. Empathy fosters a deeper connection and shows genuine concern.

14. **Show Affection:** Physical touch, kind words, or acts of service are ways to express affection and honor in a relationship. These gestures affirm your care for the other person.

15. **Be Honest and Transparent:** Open communication builds trust. Be honest about your thoughts and feelings and encourage them to do the same.

Incorporating these tips into your relationship can create an environment of honor and mutual respect.

CHAPTER 9:
WE HAVE BEEN DOING IT ALL WRONG!

We've been approaching it all wrong! Sometimes, people's perceptions of marriage differ from what they envisioned. Some think the husband is in charge, and the wife follows. Others live by the adage, "Happy wife, happy life," which implies that the husband mindlessly serves the wife's every whim. But when we look back, marriage was meant for both partners to support and help each other.

Have you ever thought about your marriage mission? Have you and your spouse or future spouse talked about what you want your marriage to be like? It's crucial to figure out where you both see yourselves going. A marriage mission helps set expectations about your roles in your marriage. Being a parent has taught me a lot. When I became a dad, I thought my child would do things as I expected just because I was her dad. But many people approach marriage with a similar idea – "I'm the husband, and my wife should know that I love her."

We need to talk to each other to expect things to happen as we want them to. We often feel disappointed because we expect things without talking about them. Men and women usually don't see marriage in the same way. They love each other and want to live together, but their expectations and needs can differ.

If you need more clarification on my perspective, talk to a man about to get married. He might be excited and a bit nervous. He's happy to be with the woman he loves but might not cry tears of joy. Now, a woman's response might be different. While she could feel the same way, there's a good chance her eyes might get a little teary.

We need to fully grasp that marriage is a partnership, a connection where two individuals work towards being a united whole. How do you blend two different sets of ideas, views, and thinking methods into a smooth unity? The answer is simple: through cooperation. Yes, I said it! It's not just about one person submitting; it's about both partners submitting to each other. Like any team or organization, both parties must work together with a shared mission and support that mission to make progress. This unity may look different from one household to another, but the basic idea remains the same – the relationship needs care, effort, and collaboration. The growth comes from both partners aiming for a greater good beyond themselves.

Having faith doesn't mean that everything magically happens for you. Because it doesn't, it means believing you have your partner and are enabled as you do the work. A strong relationship might seem unconventional. We may seem foolish when we do things that are not common, but that's what having faith is all about. Faith becomes the foundation for two people to come to and work well in a marriage. You might wonder why that is. It's because you have two people with different perspectives joining together. That's not something that happens naturally. Could that be why many marriages face challenges? Sometimes, we approach marriage as if it's a regular thing, but in reality, marriage is spiritual. And when it comes to spiritual things, faith is the key.

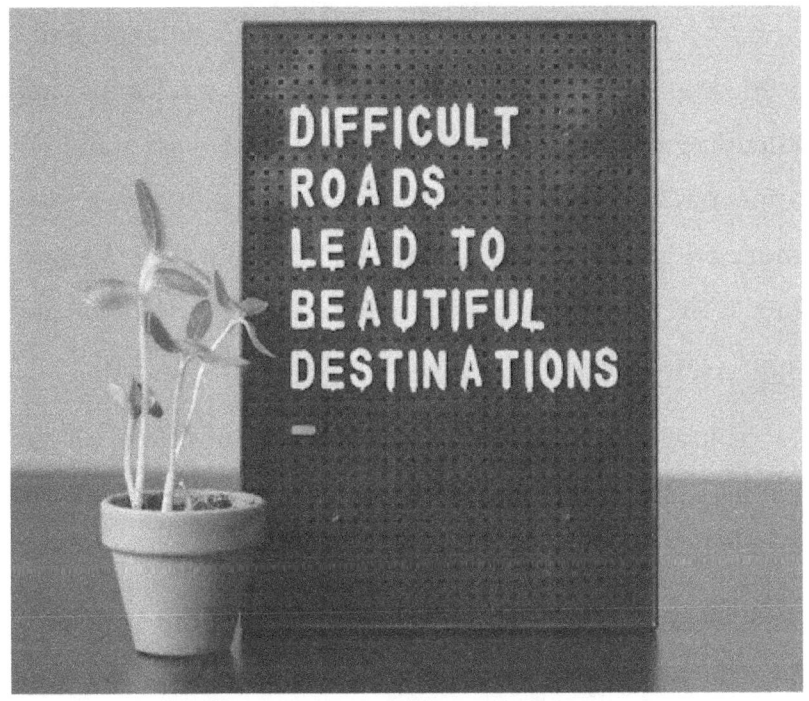

Marriage is like a promise of love. It's not just about how you feel. While feelings of acceptance, affirmation, closeness, and passion are essential, the core value is love! Love goes beyond these feelings and shows the strength and effort you're willing to put in because you promise love. According to Webster's Dictionary, love is a feeling of strength or constant affection for a person.

1 Corinthians 13 reminds us that love is patient and kind and doesn't keep a record of wrongs. But we must keep reminding ourselves of this because the person we love is

human, and their humanity shows up unexpectedly. Understanding what love truly means guides us and encourages us when life gets tough. As time passes and our appearance changes, the promise of love becomes even more critical. Your partner will undergo physical changes, but it is the inner person whom we are to love and appreciate most.

Many of our problems result from mistakes or bad habits. The challenge is that we often want to avoid admitting these issues.

The real issue is when we need to face our problems. Instead of fighting or avoiding them, if we ask the right questions before reacting, we can respond more effectively. The first question should be to ourselves. Since many people don't usually look inward, we often react as if the problem is external. The first question we should ask ourselves when facing challenges is, "Is there anything too hard for me to handle?" The answer is a definite NO! So, we need to look at ourselves, understand our emotions, and learn from what we face.

Hurt usually comes from inside us. I am referring to emotional and mental hurt. How we interpret and experience things makes us feel a certain way. Viewing marriage as a covenant means seeing the couple as a united entity, with equal power and authority, working together. Marriage is choosing to be with the person, even if it means being unhappy together instead of happy alone. When we promise to prioritize each other above all, it starts with putting aside our desires.

Please know that I am not saying that you should lose yourself in the relationship, nor am I saying that you need to suck it up and suffer through it. How is that the right thing for you? I remember a time and place where I sacrificed my identity for the sake of pleasing my partner. I am a very outgoing person. That's what she loved about me. However, once coupled in marriage, that outgoing person who she loved shined a light on her insecurities. Guess what, the relationship didn't last! Why? Because I have more to offer when I am not carrying the weight of falsehood. I would avoid talking to certain people because she found it offensive. If it was flirtatious, I could understand, but it was not. I am much happier and more willing to give when I can be myself.

When we talk about marriage, people see it in two main ways. One is the covenant view, tied to religious and cultural traditions. It sees marriage as a sacred promise between people and God. The other view is more modern, where marriage is a partnership based on personal happiness and mutual agreement.

The covenant view, often rooted in religion, sees marriage as a sacred and lasting promise. It's not just a legal or social deal; it's a deep commitment with spiritual significance. In this view, marriage is a journey where a couple grows spiritually together, and the commitment is considered sacred and unbreakable.

On the other hand, modern society views marriage differently. In our modern society, marriage is a practical partnership. People marry for personal happiness and compatibility and to achieve their goals. The focus here is on individual freedom and satisfaction, sometimes leading to questions about the need for a lifelong commitment.

The covenant view believes in a higher purpose for marriage. In this view, the couple is accountable to God rather than just to each other. This sense of accountability strengthens commitment and makes couples more resilient in facing challenges. In modern society, marriage is a contract that can be adjusted or ended if things don't work out.

However, despite these differences, there are some common threads. Both views recognize the need for companionship, shared experiences, and emotional support. They also agree that communication, trust, and respect are crucial for a healthy relationship.

> *Assessing seed is challenging because it compels us to confront our faults, risking exposure to others.*

When we engage our faults, we learn the importance of trust in any relationship. Trust forms the bedrock of a strong connection and serves as the gateway to genuine intimacy. True intimacy flourishes in the fusion of authenticity and trust—an "into me see" experience where one presents one's authentic self to be seen by one's partner. However, our flaws hinder our ability to live vulnerably and trust others.

The dating process comes with numerous challenges, even for the most discerning individuals. Grown-ups date with a purpose, seeking meaningful connections. Once we clearly understand ourselves, we can formulate a list outlining what aligns with our needs and values. This list serves as a guide, highlighting areas where we can extend and receive grace in building a connection.

Thinking of marriage as a covenant, not just a contract, is crucial for a lasting relationship. A covenant is an enduring promise. Seeing marriage as a covenant means you now benefit from infinite possibilities and joy that will last a lifetime. It's not just about sticking together when things are easy – it's a promise to stick together through all the hard times, too. Marriage as a covenant doesn't view the relationship as a contract with a termination clause for this reason or that reason: It's a promise made before God that binds the couple together beautifully and mysteriously.

Covenantal marriages often involve a spiritual side, such as a shared belief or higher purpose. This spiritual connection adds something unique to the relationship, giving it common ground and a bigger picture to guide it through life.

Contracts have rules, but covenants are all about the long run. Seeing marriage as a covenant means thinking about the future. You're in it for the long haul, ready to work on your relationship and improve it over time. Covenantal marriages focus on growing and supporting each other. It's not just about being together; it's about both of you becoming better individuals. This mindset helps you invest in each other's personal growth and create a positive environment for both of you.

Marriage, the profound intertwining of lives, defies conventional understanding. It's not merely a social and legal institution but a dynamic and transformative journey where two distinct individuals embark on a covenanted shared path.

The notion that a marital union requires a shared vision is not novel, but it's a truth that often overshadows societal expectations. Consider the metaphor of a ship setting sail – a clear destination and a collaborative effort to navigate the waters are essential. Similarly, a marriage without a defined mission can drift aimlessly, lose direction, and never achieve its maximal potential of a loving union. If worse, it becomes susceptible to external pressures and internal conflicts.

One practice that I found beneficial and fun was check-in time! Check-in time was when we would go out to neutral territory. Typically, in a date(ish) environment, we speak truthfully about how we felt and what's going on in our lives and celebrate that we made it to the next check-in! If you have been in any relationship, you understand that it is work worthy of celebrating. The fundamental purpose of checking in time is to isolate us from day-to-day pressure and responsibilities so we can listen and share with our partners. This little effort gives you quality time, strengthens the bond, and changes the mood if you do it right. I will leave the rest for you to ponder.

Communication is the cornerstone of establishing and sustaining a shared mission in marriage. Expectations, when left uncommunicated or poorly expressed, can lead to disappointment. Make sure you communicate your expectations. Your spouse needs to know. If your spouse is anything like me, that crystal ball is sometimes cloudy. Unspoken expectations based on traditional gender roles can sow seeds of misunderstanding, hindering the organic growth of the marital bond.

Remembering that marriage is a covenant that will help the partners decide who likes what responsibility best and even honestly assess who does what best. I shouldn't be responsible for the money if I love numbers but can't balance a checkbook. We'd suffer in our finances unless I became a pupil and allowed my partner to teach me. Likewise, old-school traditions believe that a female should cook, but we need to switch responsibilities if I'm a chef, love cooking, and can't boil an egg. I'm not ready to have a boiled egg-only diet.

It's crucial to recognize that men and women often bring different perspectives, emotions, and expectations to the marital table. The content suggests that mutual submission is the key to reconciling these differences and fostering a harmonious union. Here, submission is not a one-sided act but a mutual surrender to the covenant and mission. It's about aligning individual goals and aspirations with the covenant and tilling the marital ground for proper germination and growth of the covenant seed.

The content subtly introduces faith as integral to a thriving marriage—belief in the potential for growth, understanding, and resilience within the marital bond, not faith in the divine sense.

Life can be unpredictable, and marriages face challenges. Seeing your marriage as a covenant gives you stability during tough times. It reminds you of the commitment and shared values that can help you through anything. Covenantal marriages go beyond the basics. They create a deep emotional connection where you both feel secure and valued. The commitment to the covenant makes room for emotional intimacy, strengthening your relationship.

In a love covenant, these aspects of love are not just ideals but practical principles that guide the commitment and effort invested in the marital relationship.

Challenges, a natural part of any relationship, are viewed through self-reflection and introspection. Let's be honest here, and don't feel obligated to share the answer. Have you ever wondered why I did that? I know I say that too frequently. Asking myself that question implies that I have a conflict or challenge based on a previous thought or position. There you have it! Proof that all relationships have challenges. If you have challenges within yourself, surely adding another person to the equation won't make it easier. But it will be more enjoyable once you practice the art of learning and then laughing. Reflection and introspection encourage a shift from reactive responses to contemplative inquiry. Asking, "Is there anything too hard for God?", "What could I do to make this better?" or "What could I have done to trigger this?" or "What does he/she need from me now?" redirects the focus inward, prompting individuals to seek their true reflection and understand their emotional resilience. This approach aligns with the original intention of marriage – to create a union reflecting a harmonious collective entity with equal power and authority.

Hurt, a common byproduct of challenges, originates internally. Never forget that all hurt isn't bad. Have you ever heard of a concept called growing pains? That is what I am talking about here. Hurt that comes from experiencing something new or different. Emotional hurt is a translation of perceived or experienced sensations into emotional responses. The original intention for marriage is not a solitary pursuit of happiness but a commitment to endure hardships with a partner. The vow to forsake all others is not just a commitment to exclusivity but an initial act of self-denial, a recognition that individual needs must yield to the collective well-being of the union. Here is a news flash from my past. You will not always like your partner, and I know you are one of God's most fabulous creations, but you, too, my friend, are not always loveable. That's why there needs to be a covenant to sustain us in our unlovable state.

Thinking of marriage as a covenant completely reshapes how you understand your relationship. It adds depth, purpose, and a strong commitment, making your marriage a solid and lasting journey. Couples embark on a journey of intentional love, mutual respect, and unwavering faith. It beckons them to cultivate a love that transcends fleeting emotions, a respect that goes beyond societal expectations, and a faith that propels them through life's storms. In doing so, the content paints a portrait of marriage not as a static institution bound by tradition but as a dynamic and evolving journey. In this sacred covenant, two individuals merge into one united entity.

One of the reasons this book is entitled The Marriage Seed is that I love gardening. My yard is like my sanctuary. There is something about it that feeds my soul. In my garden, I have all types of plants. Some are annuals, and others are perennials. I hope you can learn from my embarrassment. It took me several years to go into garden centers and ask what the difference was before I truly understood. Now, I can help you. Annuals have a short life cycle. They look great for one season, die off, and never grow again.

On the other hand, we have perennials that grow back year after year. While you may be happy that perennials return year after year, we must also acknowledge that they tend to have shorter blooming periods. In dating, the long blooms of an annual plant are pleasing. But its beauty will soon end and never return. On the other hand, perennials may bloom less during the first year, but their nature is to bloom again and again. Perennials provide more permanent and sustainable beauty.

> *In my marriage, I seek perennials—guaranteed beauty as a fixed part of the journey.*

This mindset turns your marriage into a meaningful adventure, where you and your partner face life with a shared purpose and a promise to stick by each other's side—guiding the relationship toward a deeper, more meaningful connection and continuing the journey, carrying the wisdom embedded in these words, forging ahead into the uncharted territories of our shared missions, weathering storms with grace, and building a legacy of love that stands the test of time. Any other ending to your relationship isn't optional and is contrary to your covenant.

CHAPTER 10:
FERTILIZE: DROP THE F-BOMB!

When you think of dropping the F-bomb, what comes to mind? Answer out loud only if you're alone. Most people get whiplash when they hear someone dropping the F-bomb. Not only will people look often, but they'll judge you for doing it. Here is where I'd like you to learn some new words. Are you ready? Say it with me!

The F-bomb I'm talking about is FORGIVENESS! Forgiveness is essential because you are stuck in that moment or event if you don't forgive. When you're in a relationship, if you can't drop the F-bomb when you're offended, your relationship will be unable to grow beyond your ability to move forward. Without forgiveness, it is difficult for an offended person to move beyond where they were hurt emotionally. Therefore, even if you stay in a relationship for 2, 4, 7, or even 50 years, you and the relationship are stuck and won't progress to its full potential if the offense is still lurking. Dropping the F-bomb enables you to continue growing. Forgiveness can liberate your mind to process your next move with clarity and wisdom. Dropping the F-bomb starts the healing required to disarm your emotions from dictating how to handle the offense. The F-bomb gives access to understanding and clarity.

Forgiveness is an art often overlooked but crucial for a lasting connection. Notice that I said forgiveness is an art. I did not say that it was an action. Art expresses human creative skill and imagination, usually expressed visually, producing works recognized primarily for their beauty or emotional power. Forgiveness draws partners closer

Fertilize: Drop the F-bomb!

emotionally while simultaneously reflecting the true beauty of the covenant union. The seed of forgiveness is artistic. Imagine this art form not as a sturdy bridge but as a delicate garden cultivated with intention, understanding, and a willingness to let go.

One thing I am grateful for is that I learned to forgive early in life. I'm not a saint, but I learned to forgive because unforgiveness keeps you in the forefront and under a microscope. There is no need to hold someone to a standard I can't keep. I have so much dirty laundry I need to let you clean your own. I'll probably need forgiveness for something I said, did, or thought.

Picture forgiveness as the soil where both partners plant seeds of empathy and understanding, cultivating a garden of resilience and compassion. In this section, we explore the transformative power of forgiveness in relationships, offering insights into how this gardening process can mend ruptures and fortify the emotional fabric of your connection. Are you feeling creative or artistic yet?

> *Forgiveness doesn't erase the past; instead, it shifts the focus from the hurt to healing.*

We help you acknowledge pain without letting it dictate your relationship's narrative. The blueprint isn't a rigid plan but a heartfelt conversation about forgiveness's liberating effects and the freedom it brings to both individuals.

Now, imagine forgiveness as a garden, where seeds of understanding grow into vibrant plants, connecting hearts capable of weathering any storm. Forgiveness tends to breed gratefulness; when someone is grateful, they are usually more appreciative and honored. I don't know you; maybe you already have too much honor in your relationship. As we navigate this metaphorical garden, we share anecdotes of couples who have embraced the art of forgiveness, turning moments of strife into opportunities for growth. Letting go of resentment, fostering empathy, and cultivating an environment where mistakes are acknowledged, learned from, and forgiven. Through practical examples and heartfelt narratives, we invite you to see forgiveness as a skill that, when honed, contributes to the longevity and vitality of your relationship.

The art of forgiveness isn't about perfection but progress. We discuss the nuances of offering and seeking forgiveness, emphasizing that vulnerability and humility are the brushes that paint the most profound strokes on the canvas of love. The tone remains conversational, reassuring you and your partner that forgiveness is a shared journey, an evolving art form that transforms with each stroke. Priceless!

We impart a sense of hope, assuring you that, like any art, forgiveness becomes more refined and enriching over time.

THREE KINDS OF PROBLEMS YOU'LL ENCOUNTER THAT NEED FORGIVENESS AND CONFLICT RESOLUTION

Solvable problems include house cleaning, disciplining children, sex, and in-laws. Solvable problems for one couple can involve the same topics that could be perpetual problems for a different couple. A solvable problem within a relationship is situational. The conflict is simply about that topic, and each partner's position may not have a deeper meaning. A solution can be found and maintained.

Fundamental differences in personalities or lifestyle needs cause perpetual problems. All couples have perpetual problems. These issues are about the same topics as what might be solvable for another couple; however, unlike a solvable problem, they are the problems that a couple will repeatedly return to.

Gridlocked perpetual problems are perpetual problems that have been mishandled and have essentially calcified into something "uncomfortable." When a couple tries to discuss a gridlocked issue, it can feel like they are spinning their wheels and getting nowhere. The nature of gridlock is that hidden agendas underlie the problem.

There is very little difference between the problems of a successful relationship and a failed relationship. The issue is that people are the problem; wherever you have people, you will have a problem. Every person carries with them problems. You may not be able to notice them, but if you get close enough for a long enough time, they will reveal themselves. After all, no one is perfect!

> *Healthy relationships understand that conflict is normal*

Healthy relationships understand that conflict is normal, and they find ways to navigate through their complex challenges and progress forward. Unhealthy relationships never get past those conflicts, and those conflicts become dead ends. If you're reading this book, I would like to believe that you want a healthy relationship. When my relationship was failing, I sought counseling! The reason I sought counseling was because I knew that there was an issue or conflict. The problem is I didn't know how to articulate the issues in a way that would help resolve them. I needed help! So, I sought help. Also, note that I said the relationship was failing, the ties being how we related. The perception of the conflicts and hurt was more significant than our bond. Sad, but true. When you cannot see around the proverbial corner of the conflict, the more substantial influence wins.

QUESTIONS TO FORM A HEALTHY FOUNDATION FOR CONFLICT RESOLUTION

Who do you serve?

Remember the hierarchy of who you serve in life to have a healthy foundation for conflict resolution. First, of course, is God, but then, it's your spouse! Their needs come before anyone else's. Serving your spouse is how God created it to be, and He has done so because this is how we best take care of one another in marriage. When you are committed to serving your spouse above all, you will work with them instead of against them in conflict resolution.

Whom do you submit to?

As hard as submission can be, we must submit to our spouses. While it sounds like a painful negative thing, we must not consider it that way. Submitting to our spouse is a powerful expression of love, commitment, and dedication to what's best for our spouse. No matter how unified you are, there will be times when you need to submit to your spouse's needs over your own. In doing so, you love them in remarkable ways.

Whom will you sacrifice for?

Marriage comes with sacrifice. It's as simple as that. If you're unwilling to sacrifice in marriage, you will never be successful in conflict resolution. There are times that the needs of your spouse, or the needs of the marriage as a whole, will trump your own, and you'll have to sacrifice something.

Whom will you sow into?

Sowing into our spouses helps them feel loved, empowered, and unique. We must learn our spouses' love language and feed into them in meaningful ways. The more we build into our spouses, the more we will calm the potential for conflict. Sowing into our spouses creates a loving, peaceful environment without contention.

What is your decision-making process?

Do you and your spouse have a mutually understood decision-making process you follow? If not, it's a beneficial tool that will help in many aspects of your marriage. Life is a series of decisions, big and small. The decisions you make will shape your life and marriage. That's why you must have a decision-making process as a couple. A process like this will help ensure you're on the same page in your decisions and give you a clear direction to follow when the path ahead isn't apparent.

This decision-making process also helps quiet the potential for conflict by setting a standard for making decisions as a couple. Instead of coming at a decision from two different perspectives and clashing because of it, you will already understand how you will approach that process.

Who do you respect?

Respect goes an incredibly long way in every relationship. Where there is no respect, there is a lack of trust, intimacy, and growth in a marriage. It's your responsibility to help your spouse feel empowered, respected, and like a contributing member of the relationship. Let your spouse know they are integral to your life and that your marriage is an authentic, equal partnership.

How do you respond when things don't go your way?

We can't always control what happens in our marriage, but we CAN control how we react to it. There will be times when things don't go our way. We may have envisioned things going one way or the other, but suddenly, they veer in the opposite direction. That's OK! It can be disappointing and challenging to deal with our emotions, but we must learn to also react with love, peace, and grace. No matter how disappointed, hurt, confused, or frustrated we feel by a particular chain of events, it's NEVER an excuse to treat our spouse with anything but love, respect, and kindness.

How do you respond to financial hardships?

Financial hardships have been the cause of many marital conflicts. Sadly, finances remain atop many lists of the leading causes of divorce. But it doesn't have to be that way! Sadly, when financial hardships come, many people attack their spouse, spending habits, etc. Instead of doing that, which is NEVER fruitful, we must strategize with our spouses on how to better handle finances and find a better path as we advance. Instead of being a time of tension and conflict, financial hardships can serve as an opportunity to strengthen your marriage as you work through them!

Resolving conflict means explicitly expressing the difference between two individuals, and its success depends entirely on the ability of both parties to express their differences as strongly as possible. We must understand that there is a difference between a disagreement and a misunderstanding. A disagreement is when there is understanding but not agreement on the experience. A misunderstanding requires more knowledge regarding what the person is trying to say, meaning we need clarity on the person's point or perspective.

What couples usually don't know is that we all have the unconscious fantasy that our partner will fulfill our needs. Blaming our partners causes defensiveness; they can defend themselves by fighting back or withdrawing and not communicating. Criticizing and blaming your partner is like withdrawing money from the bank of the relationship.

The most important thing to happen is a shift in our thinking. We don't realize our responsibility for what goes wrong and underestimate our ability to change the situation by changing ourselves. Instead, both partners must ask themselves, "Why is my partner's behavior or characteristics so annoying? What are my real needs, and why am I frustrated when my partner cannot fulfill them? Did I ever communicate these needs directly? Each partner needs to focus on what they can change about themselves. Instead of thinking, "I feel unsatisfied in this relationship, so you have to change," they need to start thinking, "We have a problem, so how can I approach it?"

Working on communication and conflict resolution does not lead to happier marriages. Conflict resolution is not the decisive factor as happily married couples may have a lot of conflict and may not validate when angry at each other. It is the positive sentiments overriding the negative ones.

Conflict may cause irreconcilable differences in a relationship. However, what determines a relationship's success or failure is whether the person gets more good out of it than bad. There may be more benefits than disadvantages and more areas of agreement than disagreement. Otherwise, even if two people communicate well, the relationship will only succeed if compatible.

Tips On Resolving Conflict

1. Accept whatever feelings the differences generate—helplessness, anger, disappointment, joy, anticipation—and treat them as natural and essential for both parties.

2. Listen to the other person's words and ensure you understand. If you need more communication, call a time-out.

3. Be responsible for your feelings. Others do not instill feelings in us, so blaming them for what is happening inside us is unreasonable and unhelpful.
4. Treat confronting as an exercise in rationality. It requires clarity, calmness, and patience in the presence of often strong feelings.
5. Find a resolution both parties can accept. Don't try to change the other person; work on the behavior.
6. If the issue seems unresolvable, experiment—try it one way or another and evaluate it together.
7. If you are in a pattern of miscommunication over many months, consider seeking couples therapy.
8. Don't make assumptions about your partner's motivations or behaviors. You could be way off the mark.
9. Discuss any issues as they arise, and don't let them fester into more significant problems.
10. Remember that a bit of communication and affection can go a long way.

What is Forgiveness?

The loose definition of forgiveness is "the action or process of forgiving or being forgiven." But the process of forgiveness is so much more than that. Sometimes, people must work through their pain for months or years to get closure and get on with their lives.

Almost every religion in the world teaches forgiveness. Today, psychologists and medical research have also determined that forgiveness of a wrong perpetrated against you can positively change your health and mental well-being. If for nothing else, that makes forgiveness worth pursuing. Research about forgiveness and its effect on the body and mind has blossomed in recent years. It began as a concept in some religions, and now it's known as a potent force in improving our well-being. To achieve happiness and success, dozens of inspirational books and motivational speakers include forgiveness in their "must dos" lists.

By forgiving, you're not condoning the action but shifting your thinking to let go of the powerful hold that revenge and anger have on your thoughts and actions. Any grief requires forgiveness to reach closure. It's a natural process of acknowledging the pain and loss and replacing all negative thoughts with positive ones.

You don't need to reconcile with the person to forgive. The process of forgiveness is for you alone. It's releasing the power someone has on you and getting on with your life without the nagging thoughts of revenge and anger so raw that it changes and defines you. You also don't have to forget the wrong to forgive. You need to decide how you will think about the transgression in the future and how you'll let it affect your life, if at all.

Forgiveness is also not denying the wrong or suppressing your feelings. Forgiveness involves vividly remembering the transgression without feelings of revenge or anger. Those feelings only harm you, not the person who wronged you. Justice isn't reached with forgiveness, although it's easier to forgive when the person apologizes. In many cases, justice involves punishment or compensation for the action. You should pursue forgiveness over justice. Forgiveness is never about excusing or condoning the action. When you suffer an injustice, you don't need to deny it or think your feelings are wrong. You must protect yourself from future harm and take steps that will ensure your well-being.

Forgiveness is not letting pain define who you are. The act of forgiveness is a gift to yourself. You're permitting yourself to enjoy life anyway – despite the hurt you've experienced. The mental clutter and confusion that comes from harboring the pain deep inside can end up controlling you – and control is the last thing we want to give to the person who has wronged you. You'll likely always have the memory of the pain, but not letting it control you or define you is critical to getting on with your life. Without forgiveness, you'll hold on to anger and resentment and suffer the most.

Holding on to pain can also change the course of your life. Forgiveness is difficult, but once you begin the journey, the emotional baggage you've been hanging on to will fall to the side of the road, and you'll realize how much it's been holding you back. One thing that makes forgiving someone tricky is how you may define it. You may sincerely believe that you must condone the action or turn the other cheek and pretend the horrific act didn't happen. If so, it's time to rethink how you view forgiveness.

Think about some of the following ways that forgiveness can help you get on with your life:

- Forgiveness helps you move on from hurt and heartache to happiness.
- You'll choose peace and happiness over anger when forgiving.
- Provides energy previously used to hold on to resentment and anger.
- Forgiveness lets you eliminate negative thoughts plaguing your mind and soul.
- You're given a blank slate to write your future.

When you let the pain of past transgressions keep you from moving on with your life in a positive way, you remain chained to the past. Those old hurts will hang on forever and change your life's path. Forgiveness allows you to leave the hurt just where it needs to be—in the past—and gives you clarity and happiness for the future.

When someone you care for – or even a stranger – does something to harm you, forgiving them can be difficult. That's especially true if the transgressor won't admit their actions or show remorse. You may think you'll never be able to forgive the person. It's hard to work through the anger, resentment, and negative thoughts of revenge. You can choose who you want to forgive and who you won't forgive. Just be sure you don't remain in a toxic trap by not knowing the difference between forgiveness and acceptance. You may never forgive the harm done to you, but you may be able to accept that it happened and continue.

It isn't easy to honor your emotions and work through to a type of acceptance, but here are some tips you may want to heed:

- Decide on the relationship you want with the other person involved. If a spouse has hurt you, keeping the marriage together may be a higher priority than if the perpetrator was a criminal or someone you didn't know well.
- Change your thought patterns. If you dwell on the negative, you'll reap a life of negativity. Stop letting the injury consume your mind by using methods such as meditation and relaxation, and take care of yourself.

- Stop thinking about "revenge." Focus on and consider the resolution (if one exists). If you don't see a resolution, put those thoughts aside and replace them with positive thoughts of the present and the future.

- Did you contribute to the transgression? You may need some deep thinking or even therapy to realize what part you played (if any) in the harm you feel was done to you. If your thinking leads you to conclude that you were partly responsible for what happened, accepting and forgiving the other person is more effortless. Don't remain trapped in an abusive or mentally harmful situation.

Take the steps you need to get on with your life and leave the abusive person behind. Staying will only bring emotional and physical stress. It isn't easy to turn a situation around and observe it from the outside looking in, but that simple act can be very revealing. How would a disinterested, third-party person see the problem?

Even though it can be very challenging to forgive someone who's hurt you so deeply, the anger and resentment can take over your entire life, cause mental, physical, and spiritual problems, and become the focus of your existence.

I had four significant intimate relationships in my life. I define a significant relationship as one that lasted more than two years. None of them ended well. Yet, all of them ended. Even if it was an amicable break-up, we invested time, effort, and resources into something and someone and will never recover the loss; it didn't end well. Anytime there is a loss, there must be a grieving process, and you're healing. That process begins with acceptance and immediately crosses over to forgiveness. Yes, I said both of my marriages were easier to apply forgiveness than my other two relationships. It was easier because we cohabitated. When you are living in a situation that is going south very fast, you see more and have a better understanding of some of the "Why?" it makes processing without finding fault easier. We lived through struggles together. That placed me in a space where I could forgive out of compassion. When you spend years in counseling and keep hitting the same roadblocks, there is a deeper issue. There came a time when I conceded that neither one of us was a bad person because the relationship did not work. After all, we had lots of fun together! Our public and non-coupled experiences were great! When I say non-coupled, I refer to the activities and experiences that didn't require us to collaborate or work together. We just weren't good teammates. Having that understanding made forgiving easier.

You may never forgive the actions against you, but you can make peace with them by accepting them and going on with your life. Revenge thinking is toxic to the mind and body. It's time to replace those thoughts with positive ones. You must ask yourself if you played a part in the harm done. Considering your role isn't easy to think about, but if you conclude that you did have something to do with the outcome, it's easier to forgive the other person.

Unless you change your thought patterns, you'll live a life of negativity, and the injury will consume your mind during your waking hours. Forgiveness doesn't come easy or quickly. It takes a commitment to see the process through and emerge healed.

> *Acknowledge your hurt and give it voice and feelings.*

Express your emotions healthily through writing, meditation, and other methods. Attempt to understand the perpetrator's mind. Think about the person's background in terms of relationships and past experiences. Can you feel empathy for them?

Empower yourself. A hurt or wrong can take away your power to cope and enjoy life to the fullest. Empower yourself by going through the steps of forgiveness. Don't stop working on yourself. Forgiveness takes time, effort, and, most of all, a commitment to the process.

What if You Can't Forgive?

Forgiveness takes time, patience, and a commitment to let go of hurt and get on with your life. But what if you can't find enough compassion and understanding about the situation to let go? When someone you trust and love hurts you, you may feel sad, angry, or develop confusion about the problem and even question yourself and if you were "good enough" to have a relationship with the person. If these grudges continue to permeate your mind, you'll have hostility that can take root in every part of your life.

Those who can't forgive have trouble being happy.

Unforgiving people allow negative and vengeful thoughts to shove out the positive thoughts of happiness and joy they may be experiencing and relive the past repeatedly. There is one thing I know, and that is that I cannot go back and fix wrongs from the past. Since it is in the past, I must choose to learn, grow, and move forward! Why waste now on yesterday? Whatever took place yesterday is history; it cannot change. Whether you realize it or not, you're keeping the hurt alive in your mind and not realizing the benefits you would have if you forgave and let it go.

If you don't cultivate forgiveness, you may risk some of the following scenarios.

- Depression and anxiety – Constant anxiety and depression can wreak havoc in every aspect of your life. It keeps you from enjoying life to the fullest, and worse, it can turn good relationships into bad ones.
- Bitterness and anger—Although you may not realize it, harboring hurt feelings can bring bitterness and anger to everything you experience, including new relationships.

- No ambition—Negative thoughts can prevent you from thinking your life has purpose or meaning, and you may have trouble meeting previous goals you've set for yourself.
- No enjoyment of the present moment – It would be a shame if you kept negative thoughts of a past situation alive and let it ruin the present moment for you. Take time to think about all you're missing because you can't let go of the past.
- Lose valuable and strong relationships – Your connectedness with others is bound to suffer if you harbor negative thoughts. Think about how blessed your life is with these people in it, and commit to changing your thoughts to positive ones by working through the process of forgiveness.

Spend time thinking and praying about what forgiveness can mean in your life. This process can bring peace, joy, and healing by removing the power from the person who hurt you and giving it back to you.

Rarely does someone hurt to wake up one morning and realize they've forgiven the perpetrator. Forgiveness, just like every worthwhile cause in your life, takes a commitment from you that you'll see the process through to realize the changes you want to make. You may want to contemplate why you need to forgive before you commit. Reflection on the situation, your reaction to it, and how it's affecting your life is essential. And it would be best if you stopped seeing yourself as a helpless victim. Decide to actively forgive (let go of the old hurts) and tell yourself that you'll forgive as soon as you're ready – and not a moment before.

HERE ARE SOME STEPS TO TAKE WHEN YOU'VE COMMITTED TO THE PROCESS OF FORGIVENESS:

Acknowledge the hurt. Understand that the transgression happened and that the transgression hurt you. Feel the inner pain you've harbored since the situation and express those emotions in a way that doesn't hurt or attack anyone.

Forgive yourself. Most people acknowledge they had some role in what happened to them, especially in relationships. Understand that role and commit to building the relationship (if salvageable). Commit to doing what you must to go on with your life.

Try to understand the perpetrator. There are so many reasons why people do bad things. Look at the situation from the perpetrator's point of view and replace the anger you feel with compassion and empathy.

Decide if you want to stay in the relationship. If you're in an abusive relationship that hasn't gotten better, maybe it's time to leave. Take care of yourself in these situations, and be sure you're safe.

Write a story of what happened to hurt you. It helps to use expressive words and write down the actual situation. Even if you haven't forgiven and moved on yet, include that scenario at the end of the story.

Analyze your thoughts. Chances are, your present hurt isn't coming from the situation but from your thought formula about what happened. Know that you control your thoughts and practice to replace the hurtful ones with happy, positive ones.

Practice stress reduction techniques. Many methods (such as Yoga) exist to help you overcome the feelings of anxiety and stress caused by what happened to you. These techniques can calm your body and mind and help put you in a state of forgiveness.

Use your energy wisely. Rather than wasting your energy on negative thoughts and actions of the past, look for ways to make yourself happy and achieve the positive goals that you've set for yourself.

Gratitude. Being thankful for what you have is an excellent way to replace negative feelings and thoughts with positive ones. Some victims claim that daily writing in a gratitude journal helps them move forward.

Empower yourself. Realize that a life well-lived is the best revenge possible, and concentrate on empowering yourself to take back control of your thoughts and actions so that you're the one who benefits.

It's your choice. Forgive or hang on to the hurt and trap yourself in a quicksand of toxicity. Holding inside feelings of hate, distrust, and anger can ruin your life and the lives of those around you. When you power through the steps of forgiveness, you're not excusing the person or the act, but you're accepting that it happened and will always be a part of you, but that it won't define you.

Acceptance of the situation can make the following positive changes in your life:

- Helps you stand up for your values.
- Helps you forgive yourself for things you might have done to hurt someone.
- Gives you clarity that isn't possible when you harbor emotional poison.

When you accept that you were hurt deeply, you can offer forgiveness as a gift to yourself. It will reduce the hurt, bring peace, and make you happy. It's a choice.

When you choose the path of non-forgiveness, you carry the heavy burden and the helplessness of being a victim. It's ironic to think that another choice – forgiveness -- could be the one to help you out of the dark hole and work out of weakness and into strength.

Studies show that people who can work through forgiveness enjoy better physical and mental health. They're not as prone to cardiovascular diseases, high blood pressure, depression, or anxiety.

Deciding to forgive and then working through the steps is difficult. You must include visualizing the situation, trying to understand the perpetrator's point of view, and vowing to forgive without benefiting yourself.

The irony is that when you forgive, you reap the most benefits. Living free from anger and resentment and concentrating on happy thoughts rather than destructive ones is truly a gift to yourself.

Also, forgiveness comes with a new pattern of doing good, being altruistic, and building self-esteem. Forgiveness lifts the burdens of anger and resentment from your mind and shoulders, making you feel light, free, and able to accomplish more.

There is a humble spirit in forgiveness that helps you forge new relationships and find happiness in things that only come with freedom. By forgiving, you're letting go of the anger while renouncing the perpetrated act. It's a spirit that helps every area of your life and opens you up to new experiences. Take the route of forgiveness if you find yourself harboring mistrust, animosity, and hatred for someone. It's not easy, but it's worthwhile and can be the catalyst that helps you succeed.

CHAPTER 11: FERTILIZE IT!

A garden filled with thriving plants brings joy to the gardener's heart. In the sacred garden of relationships and marriage, spiritual intimacy is an intertwining root that anchors the connection between partners. Since most people have some sense of spirituality, I'd be remiss if I didn't address the benefits of spiritual unity. If you don't believe in a deity, the principles mentioned in this book can be supported scientifically and as historical facts. Unity of the spirit or soul of a person emphasizes the shared values and beliefs that deepen the marital bond. I encourage couples to explore their spiritual journeys and foster a connection that transcends the material realm. The realm that connects your mind, will, and emotions with the invisible.

Sowing spiritual intimacy involves shared rituals, prayers, and reflections that align with the couple's belief system. Partners learn to respect and honor each other's spiritual path, creating an environment where the roots of faith and unity intertwine. As couples nurture spiritual intimacy, their connection flourishes with a profound sense of purpose and alignment.

In the well-tended spiritual garden of intimacy, the culmination lies in the joyous harvest of the fruits brought through their connection. This movement nurtures emotional, physical, intellectual, and spiritual intimacy, reaping the rewards of a bountiful and fulfilling connection. Couples are encouraged to reflect on the richness of their shared experiences and celebrate the love that has blossomed.

No matter the temperature of my marriage, having a spiritual connection was the best fertilizer! Our spiritual connection nourished our souls and minds. It was often after prayer, time alone in meditation, that I could quiet the inner attorney or the offended party long enough to see clearly. There is one thing that I can count on, and that is hearing a still, small voice when I seek peace. Typically, the voices from emotional pain are not small. That's when I knew I needed to listen. When I sow the seed of wisdom, I know it will produce a much better harvest than acting out on my feelings.

Harvesting the fruits of intimacy involves gratitude, acknowledgment, and cherishing the moments that have contributed to the flourishing connection. These spiritual acts strengthen the emotional connection with one's partner, which some call soul ties. Partners bask in the beauty of their well-tended garden, recognizing the depth and strength that have grown from intentional care and mutual investment. As couples celebrate the bountiful harvest, they affirm the resilience and beauty of their soulful and spiritual union.

This intentional journey transforms the garden of marriage into a flourishing oasis of love, passion, understanding, and unity. Couples cultivate a connection that withstands the test of time by planting the seeds of emotional, physical, intellectual, and spiritual intimacy. Not only will you see the blossoms with the vibrancy of a well-nurtured garden, but the invisible roots are even more profound than what we see on the surface. The roots enable all life to withstand the test of time and endure whatever comes.

Faith emerges as a super-fertilizing force in marriage's journey of weathering storms. Godly or Biblical marriage concepts may seem unconventional in a world that often prioritizes individualism, but they align with scientific truths. Marriage, viewed as a love covenant, requires faith—an acknowledgment that God empowers, equips, and supports the couple in their endeavors. Even those who don't believe in a deity can agree that faith is required when you start your relationship, as no one knows what they will encounter on this journey.

The unconventional nature of a Godly marriage challenges societal norms, encouraging couples to view their union as a natural occurrence and a spiritual representation created by God. This shift in perspective instills a sense of purpose beyond individual desires, emphasizing a higher good for a higher cause. Regardless of their spiritual beliefs, most people agree that entering into a marriage should improve the quality of your life.

In the book of Jeremiah, God declares, "I know the plans I have for you, plans to bring you hope and a future." Jeremiah received these encouraging words during Judah's period of enslavement. The message urged them to understand the Lord's intentions and encouraged them to build lives, form families, marry, and engage meaningfully in society—all while facing challenging circumstances. We have to make a habit of fertilizing positivity. While fertilizing circumstances or tilling the environment may not resemble the promise, knowing the instructions and principles will work.

Despite external challenges and the perception that it might be too late, the core message remains crystal clear – keep moving forward! Why? Because in marriages and relationships, the journey continues regardless of feelings or ongoing obstacles. Once planted, the seed will grow. However, dedicated efforts and nurturing are crucial for it to flourish in fertile ground.

The Song of Solomon uses vivid pictures to describe love. Even though the language might seem strange to us now, it makes more sense when considering the time. Phrases like a woman feeling special to marry a man compared to a gazelle or a man wanting a woman like a deer show deep feelings rather than just talking about looks. One of my favorite phrases in the poetic discourse says,

Fertilize it!

In many marriages today, the challenge is to take more time to reflect. Living in a fast-paced era, we often overlook the importance of sitting down, thinking about our relationships, and gaining a deeper understanding of our desires. Fertilizing relationships requires us to pause, assess the condition of the ground, and understand how to nurture and enhance their growth.

When was the last time you took a moment to reflect on your love, your beloved? In those quiet moments, we often notice things we might overlook in the busyness of daily life. Reflecting on the beauty of a thing allows us to describe it, and when defined, it becomes natural and holds significance. So, what do you see when you look at yourself? What impression do you want others to have when they think of you?

Here's an invaluable advice: "Don't rush love." Presenting yourself authentically and being available while understanding that growth may happen at different paces and seasons is essential. Rushing the process can lead to resentment and unnecessary problems. This rush becomes self-sabotaging, as it brings conflict to the relationship.

Fertilize it!

Remember that it all started with one seed or two seeds growing together. Seeds take time to develop. You've probably heard it said, "You can't rush a good thing." That has never been truer than in our relationships!

You might not have planted anything in a long time. In many cases, planting one seed isn't enough; you plant several seeds to get one plant, a single germination. This concept parallels your marriage – it's grown in the soil of commitment and deserves the effort to produce something great. The key is cultivation. Are you actively nurturing and cultivating your marriage?

Take a moment to contemplate what your love means to you. How do you see them, and how do you want them to see you? Reflecting on this can be a powerful exercise in understanding and strengthening the bond within your relationship.

Interestingly, when God spoke to Jeremiah in Jeremiah 29:11, He addressed Judah. God wanted them to submit to Nebuchadnezzar to maintain and sustain Judah. The promise was clear: If they submitted to Babylon, the city, palaces, and temples would be preserved. God didn't want the town ruined just because they refused to submit. Even if the directions you received didn't seem right, God emphasized the importance of starting afresh. If Judah had not followed the proper path, destruction would have resulted.

This lesson parallels our marriages. Just as God instructed Judah to settle down, marry, have daughters and sons, and continue life even in captivity, the same principle applies. You can't put life on hold while feeling held captive. Nobody wants a marriage that feels like it lasts 70 years, but the advice remains—keep living and producing even within challenging circumstances.

In marriage, facing tough times might change how we approach things, but the key is to keep living and loving. God didn't tell us to wait or think about being saved; He encouraged us to live as usual. Even if your spouse acts differently, stick to doing the right thing. It's God's protective power that stops everything from falling apart. Divorce leads to devastation, and God's plan for us involves navigating challenges with His guidance. So, when things feel uncertain, trust that God knows His plans for you, even when you're feeling lost.

Fertilize it!

Sometimes, words alone can't capture situations well; that's when we need to create mental images. They say a picture is worth a thousand words, and having a visual representation speaks louder than words. So, when we imagine scenes and scenarios, we tap into a powerful way of understanding.

When we deliberately think about these mental pictures, we pay attention to what's essential—making our marriage work and sharing our goals. It's like zooming in on the most crucial parts of our relationship and life journey, helping us see and understand things even when words can't fully explain them.

> *Fertilizing relationships requires us to pause, assess the condition of the ground, and understand how to nurture and enhance their growth.*

CHAPTER 12: WHAT'S IN THE SOIL?

Testing the soil before planting is highly beneficial. It helps determine the soil's nutrient levels, pH balance, and overall health, ensuring the right conditions for plant growth. By understanding what the soil needs, you can add the appropriate amendments, such as lime or fertilizers, to optimize plant health and improve yields. Soil testing also prevents over-fertilization, saving time and money and reducing environmental impact.

I once thought it was impossible to over-fertilize soil if I used organic fertilizers. My thoughts were not inaccurate, but over-fertilizing isn't necessarily beneficial. It may cause more growth, but does the improved and speedy growth produce better roots? Maybe. Over-fertilizing costs more than necessary.

What's In The Soil?

> *Soil testing in a garden is equivalent to testing and learning about your potential partner's character.*

It also helps us know more about the soil's overall health because some nutrient deficiencies are invisible to the naked eye.

Soil testing involves removing soil from its standard space, allowing it to dry out, and then separating it to see what's in it. Character sampling, like soil sampling, will enable us to see your perspective partner so you can be better prepared for how the relationship will grow.

Learning the characteristics and strengths of your partner will help you identify areas where you can feed the areas of their deficiencies.

The Book of Ruth offers valuable ideas for building great relationships. It shares principles that work whether you're dating or already in a relationship. Many people, especially women, want a relationship like Ruth and Boaz. Even if that perfect person is unavailable, we can still learn important lessons from the story.

It is crucial to focus on more than just how things were different back then. Unlike many old marriages, where families arranged things, today's relationships often involve pursuing someone you desire. The key is realizing that this pursuit may take different forms, shapes, and approaches, but it will always include agreement, acceptance, loyalty, honor, humility, and desire.

What made those old marriages work was the mindset they started with. Couples had already decided they wanted to get married, not in a negative way, with malice or selfish intent, but with the belief that they were valuable and worth the effort. They were ready to do whatever it took to keep their relationship strong.

Before I go any further, let me provide a cliffnote narrative on Boaz and Ruth's story. How will you know if you want Boaz if you don't know anything about him? Or, why should you consider a Ruth mindset when the only Ruth you know gets on everyone's nerves? Every time you see her, you shake your head, thinking she acts old and miserable, and that's the last thing anyone would want. She may even smell like she hasn't showered since biblical days. I know that was wrong, but there could be some truths; I don't know, so I will tell you a little about the dynamic duo I am referring to.

There was this lady that was married, and her husband passed away. Based on the context of her story, she was relatively young. I know this because she was still in her early childbearing stages. She was so young that she eventually had children, but what positioned her to have a great family life and the right partner to find her was the discipline of choosing to enjoy and learn during her period of purposeful singleness. Ruth was loyal, a hard worker, discerning, nurturing, selfless, and, most importantly, focused. She was so focused and faithful that she operated within her divine assignment as a daughter-in-law, making sure the mother of her dead husband was safe and needed nothing. She was blind to the fact that Boaz was checking her out. I never recommend going through life in a state of naivety, but in this case, it worked to our advantage. When Ruth's mother-in-law discovered that she caught Boaz's attention while farming, she was at her best. Not! The first advice her mother-in-law gave her was to go and wash. That's sad! But it showed she focused more on her purpose than being a lure. Now, let's talk Boaz. I'm going to keep this part short. You probably don't need to know much more than that he was a very successful businessman, had a seat and influence amongst politicians, and operated in both arenas well. He was strategic, influential, and honored while living virtuously during his singleness. For those who need to hear it like this, Boaz wasn't broke and was not a player.

Does Boaz sound like someone a woman wouldn't see? I don't think so! Especially if you're picking scraps from outside of his organization.

Ruth was emotionally and relationally in a good space. She was teachable and set on being a wife who helped while learning or leading. Boaz was handling business and saw something he lacked and wanted. Neither one needed the other for completion but desired the other for companionship and affection. They were whole as individuals and, therefore, safe to connect.

Why do so many people talk about and look for Boaz when they still need to follow Ruth's path? Let's go a little deeper. The story opens with the history of Ruth's heritage, which she left due to loyalty to Naomi. Her husband was dead. So, she went to all her family and those with emotional and biological influence over her to walk in her purpose. She did that to serve Naomi and her God. She

What's In The Soil?

wasn't looking for Boaz: She was walking in her set purpose.

Walking in your purpose with the primary goal of finding your "Boaz" raises an essential question about staying true to your authentic purpose. Think about the principle of the first mention: Adam was working when God brought Eve to him. Reflect on your journey – are you on a quest to find an Adam, Ruth, or Boaz, or are you simply embracing the path where God has led you?

A seed of marriage planted properly will reside in the latter scenario. The seed of marriage germinates best in fertile and prepared soil. It grows in a garden, not by shopping around or acting solely based on your desires within that garden. The focus shifts from actively searching for a specific person to faithfully caring for the garden where God places you.

If we're patient and align ourselves with our purpose, the gardener will remove the weeds and thorns to create a safe and healthy environment for growth. Caring for the garden through weeding, trimming, edging, and feeding will enhance and beautify it. We often try to plant ourselves and pull out weeds, which exposes our roots. Without healthy roots, the rest of the plant suffers.

I've read stories of the successful separation of Siamese twins, while others remained closely connected at vital organs, making separation virtually impossible without causing harm. Despite being distinct individuals with different brains, feelings, and emotions, they share a commonality that makes them essentially one. An attempt to separate them could be fatal because of their connection.

This analogy illustrates the connection between a husband and wife, where God calls them to be one. Although they may have different emotions, thoughts, and feelings, the essence of their unity prevails. It's like the saying, "Where the rubber meets the road," signifying their oneness. Unlike Siamese twins who are physically connected, marital unity operates more as a soul tie—a choice made within the mind and heart to commit to staying together, come what may.

The challenge arises because, unlike a physical tie, the bond in marriage is not visibly tangible. This lack of a physical tie makes it easier for couples to pull away, contributing to today's high divorce rates. A married couple must recognize that their souls, minds, and thoughts are intricately tied, not by a physical bond but by a commitment to God and a shared purpose.

In marriage, a shared purpose means that both husband and wife work together toward a common goal. This shared goal can make a big difference, changing the feel of the relationship and bringing the couple closer together.

> *When a couple has a shared purpose, they grow together.*

They support each other and get a chance to become better people. It's like going on an adventure together that helps each person grow and become their best version.

Having a shared purpose strengthens the foundation of the marriage. It goes beyond the everyday stuff and creates a deep connection. This strong foundation helps the couple face challenges and keeps the relationship steady.

When tough times come, having a shared purpose helps the couple face challenges as a team. They're not dealing with problems alone; they're doing it together, strengthening them. The shared goal acts like a compass, guiding them through tough times and bringing them closer.

A shared purpose strengthens the emotional connection between husband and wife. They share their successes, setbacks, and all the feelings that come with the journey. Shared emotional experience brings them closer, making their relationship more meaningful.

Having a shared purpose lets the couple dream about the future together. It's not just about personal goals; it's about what they want to achieve together. This shared dream inspires them, helping them overcome challenges and celebrate successes.

> *Working towards a shared purpose means the couple is thinking not just about now but also about the legacy they leave behind.*

Working towards a shared purpose means the couple is thinking not just about now but also about the legacy they leave behind. Their experiences, values, and achievements become part of their story. It's like creating a meaningful history for their family.

What's In The Soil?

Having a shared purpose brings husband and wife even closer. It's not just a goal; it's like a thread that weaves their lives together, making their journey through life more united and fuller of love.

CHAPTER 13: RANKS & STRATEGY

In our fast-paced world, it's easy to overlook the enduring impact our relationships can have. Every word spoken in love, every act of kindness, and every moment of understanding contributes to the richness of the power of relationships. It's not just about the here and now; it's about crafting a story that will be recounted with fondness by those who come after us.

The best way to create enduring love is to connect with someone with whom your soul ties—one with a comparable and compatible vantage point of life, yet uniquely different. To be clear, when I say soul. I'm referring to your mind, your will, and your emotions. I don't believe your partner needs to have or should always have the same approach. Diversity brings strength. Yet, there is no separation on what type of crops or flowers the two of you want to grow in the garden. The only way to ensure this is through communication.

The collective experiences of relationships provide data and insights. It is human nature to seek the best and simplest solutions. We uncover principles that can guide belief and behavior by studying relationship trends. With intentionality and enthusiasm, your relationship can surpass expectations by embracing these timeless principles. Just as the law of gravity keeps us grounded, approaching marriage with honesty, openness, and purpose ensures these relationship laws take effect.

Our relationships, like timeless pieces of art, have the potential to inspire others. Think of the couples whose love stories have left an indelible mark—the grandparents whose enduring love serves as a beacon of hope, the friends whose unwavering support becomes a testament to the strength of human connection. These stories become part of the collective human experience, influencing how we perceive and approach love.

Let's be mindful of the threads we weave into our relationships. Each moment and choice contributes to the larger narrative beyond our immediate circumstances. It's an invitation to be intentional architects of a tapestry that not only warms our present but also wraps future generations in the comfort of enduring love.

Ephesians 6:10-19 tells us to stand firm, draw strength from higher powers, and guard ourselves against harmful schemes. When reflecting on marriage, it's noteworthy to mention temptation didn't enter the equation until Adam had a partner. Satan existed before Eve, but he did not successfully tempt Adam to perform a destructive act until Eve arrived. Eve's arrival brought light to his needs and desires. Before Eve arrived, Adam had a singular interest and covering—a natural protection from God—that safeguarded every aspect of his being. There was very little that Adam would desire more than God's presence before Eve.

When Eve came into the picture, things changed. Emotional attachment, while good, made them vulnerable. It's imperative to point this out.

Again, I reiterate that everyone doesn't believe in a deity. Still, if you're in a relationship, you will agree that the emotional challenges are different now than when you lived in your purposeful singleness phase. To bridge the understanding of this writing better, it is not a religious book but a guide for a better quality of life. When you read God, know that it refers to all things good. When you read Satan, it insinuates all things contrary to what is good.

Now, I will continue: Satan recognized the emotional attachment and strategically targeted the institution of marriage. The absence of temptation before Eve's creation raises questions. When Adam lived a purposefully single life, he had natural protection from God, making him less vulnerable.

The introduction of Eve shifted things. Emotional attachment became a vulnerability, and Satan, recognizing this shift, targeted marriage. Acknowledging this vulnerability reinforces the importance of relying on protective measures to stand firm against harmful plots. Refusing to live a life of emotional vulnerability affects a couple's ability to share intimately. Operating within your relationship with unconditional love while operating in shame or lack of trust is impossible. Insecurity brings distance and destroys the dreams and faith you have in the potential for your relationship.

We're not fighting visible enemies but unseen evil forces. Just like a seed grows when exposed to outside elements, we must remember that these invisible forces exist. When we submit to one another, we acknowledge that our struggle isn't against our spouse but against spiritual forces and principles. Consider it: most disagreements occur when you try to incorporate an outside entity into the relationship.

> *When we acknowledge that something, or someone other than our spouse, caused the division, it changes how I manage disagreements.*

I chose to ask questions of my wife instead of being driven by the difference or disagreement.

This new way of thinking brought me several simple yet profound benefits.

- It helps us better understand the reasoning behind the decision. Knowing your partner's ways increases intimacy.
- It may reveal to us things that we have not considered

- It provides an opportunity to learn better how our partner thinks
- It may reveal an area of vulnerability or fear that needs your coverage.
- It reveals that I am not responsible for what I don't know.

It brings peace to know that the battle belongs to a higher power, and although we have roles, the victory is already secured. During the Gulf War, I fought for the United States of America, not because anyone in Iraq knew me, but through commitment. I pledged allegiance to an adversary of Iraq. Prisoners of war suffer public beatings and other types of humiliation – to weaken defenses of unity through emotional turmoil. Stay the course!

Arm yourself with God's armor to stand firm against challenges. Just like going into battle without proper protection is risky, facing life's difficulties without the right tools can be perilous. Military battles focus on providing essential tools for survival, not necessarily winning. The initiation and conclusion of a war are beyond the soldiers' control. Likewise, the battles we face in our relationships are outside of our control. All we can do is use our essential tools.

ESSENTIAL TOOLS: BUILDING A LOVE LEGACY

Creating a love legacy that transcends time necessitates purposeful actions and essential tools. As a military soldier, the fight for our relationships and marriages surpasses a quest for recognition; it strives to contribute to a reservoir of shared human experience across generations. Within relationships, deliberate actions echo with clarity, holding profound significance in strengthening a loving legacy. Consistent choices to infuse interactions with love, kindness, understanding, and empathy, even amidst life's challenges, are essential. Picture an elderly couple finding joy in simple gestures, like holding hands or sharing laughter—a testament to enduring commitment. Indeed, they have spent many days wrestling with principles and unseen/unforeseen trials that attempted to take them off course. I would love to be part of the elderly couple to which others aspire.

Similarly, a couple's journey through life's peaks and valleys becomes a beacon of hope and resilience, inspiring others in their relational journeys. Others will begin to see that while endurance comes in various forms and requires strength in differing areas, a couple's enduring faith is a principle—a law that will sustain.

Constructing a love legacy is a nuanced, ongoing process requiring dedication, mutual understanding, and a commitment to building something beyond the present moment. There is one thing I am sure most people understand: when you go into a relationship, there will be challenges. Some will come from within. Those are the times when your future self has to correct your present self, or your present self is trying to outgrow your old self. These times will be challenging for your partner. The reason I gave two examples of internal struggles is to emphasize we have more internal struggles than we have external struggles. One of my favorite things to ask others when they get upset with another is, "Have you ever changed your mind?" then I would remind them that

> *Changing your mind is simply the new you telling the old you that things have changed.*

It's an internal disagreement if you don't always agree with yourself; how can you expect to always agree with someone else? Better stated, how can you be upset when someone disagrees with you or changes their mind? Authentic love adds nutrients to your ground that strengthen your love legacy.

From everyday gestures to grand expressions of love, intentional actions shape a legacy that extends far beyond the natural realm, whether in thought or deed.

ESSENTIAL TOOLS: CULTIVATING SHARED TRADITIONS

Cultivating shared traditions acts as a compass, guiding partners through the journey of togetherness. These simple or elaborate traditions are markers along the path, providing a sense of continuity and shared history. Relationships require daily cultivation, and while we know our partners, we don't know what they are feeling unless they tell us. Standing strong with your partner against the unseen requires a compass—a tool designed to detect where they are at the core.

Shared traditions and rituals have the unique power to reinforce the bonds within a relationship. These can range from daily routines, like reading together, praying together and for each other, cooking together, or sharing a morning coffee or walk, to annual celebrations that mark significant milestones. The beauty lies in the consistency of these shared experiences, which, over time, become rooted in the essence of the relationship.

Consider the couple who revisits where they first met every year on their anniversary. The tradition transcends the act of revisiting; it becomes a pilgrimage of love, a reaffirmation of their journey together. Such traditions provide a sense of stability and a shared narrative, fostering a deep connection that withstands the test of time.

ESSENTIAL TOOLS: PRACTICAL INSIGHTS FOR MEANINGFUL TRADITIONS

Creating and sustaining meaningful traditions requires intentionality and a mutual commitment to strengthening and nurturing the relationship. Practical insights can illuminate the path for couples seeking to establish traditions that resonate with their unique connection.

- Identify Shared Interests: Explore activities that align with both partners' interests. Identifying common ground lays the foundation for meaningful traditions, whether a shared hobby, a love for nature, or a mutual appreciation for art.

- Balance Routine and Novelty: While routines provide a comforting sense of predictability, introducing novel elements can inject freshness into the relationship. Striking a balance between the familiar and the new ensures that traditions remain dynamic and engaging.

- Embrace Flexibility: Recognize that life is dynamic and circumstances may change. Flexibly adapt traditions to evolving situations, ensuring they continue to enhance rather than constrain the relationship.

- Celebrate Milestones Creatively: Big and small, offer opportune moments to establish or reinforce traditions. Get creative in commemorating these milestones, infusing them with personalized touches that reflect the essence of the relationship.

As we cultivate shared traditions, we'll uncover the profound impact these rituals can have on a relationship.

ESSENTIAL TOOLS: PASSING DOWN WISDOM

Wisdom is a gift essential for navigating the complex terrain of a relationship; it holds a distinctive value. It acts as a steady guide, complementary to the compass, offering direction through life's journey's intricate twists and turns. Couples, recognizing the profound impact of their experiences, undertake the responsibility of sharing this wisdom—a contribution that transcends the boundaries of their union.

Couples with longevity have endured seasons of challenge and profound disagreement through resilient communication and unwavering support. Sometimes, unknown principalities are the only explanation for challenging seasons. Some challenging seasons are just wicked! Disagreements over things that had no merit but caused division are wicked. Their willingness to share this narrative transforms abstract concepts like resilience and compromise into tangible, relatable experiences. Through storytelling, wisdom transcends theoretical frameworks, finding resonance in the lived realities of those who seek guidance.

As couples deliberate on the importance of passing down wisdom, they become stewards of a timeless tradition. Another relationship principle is confirmed. The lessons embedded in the fabric of their experiences shape their narrative and offer a compass to future generations embarking on the intricate voyage of love.

ESSENTIAL TOOLS: THE RIPPLE EFFECT

The impact of positive actions extends beyond the immediate sphere of the couple involved. Like a stone cast into a still pond, the ripples created by a loving and committed partnership reverberate through family, friends, and the community.

Every intentional act of love within a relationship sets a series of subtle yet potent ripples in motion. These actions, rooted in genuine care, respect, and commitment, carry an energy that transcends the confines of the couple's personal space. Whether it's a gesture of kindness, a shared moment of joy, or a collaborative effort to overcome challenges, the positivity generated becomes a force with transformative potential.

I love the water! I loved being near water since I was a child. I remember how fascinated I would get to receive the calming effects of the water. As a child, I would go to the lake in a local park and hunt for rocks. You probably guessed it; I gathered rocks to toss them across the water, trying to make them skip. If you made a rock skip properly, there would be multiple ripples. Every time the rock hit the water, what we called skipping, it created a new set of ripples. What I find ironic is the effort I spent collecting the stones; I gathered them only to toss them into the water. I loved seeing the ripples from the rocks, which are outside sources, change the water. It proved that something consistent like water can withstand and absorb a hard thing sent to disrupt its peace.

> *Your relationship, just like the water, will absorb the ripples in life and disburse the energy in the form of a ripple.*

Consider a couple that, in pursuing shared goals, inadvertently becomes a source of inspiration for friends facing relationship dilemmas. The encouragement drawn from witnessing a loving partnership in action creates a ripple effect, influencing others to invest in the quality of their relationships. Positive actions, when observed and internalized, become catalysts for change.

The ripple effect extends naturally to the immediate circles surrounding a couple. Observing the resilience and mutual support within the relationship, family members find themselves buoyed by the optimism emanating from this union. Friends, too, draw strength and inspiration from witnessing a couple navigate life's complexities hand in hand.

In essence, the positive dynamics within a relationship become a shared resource—a wellspring of encouragement and fortitude for those connected to the couple. The ripple effect transforms individual relationships within the broader network, fostering a collective love, respect, and reciprocity ethos.

As the ripples radiate outward, the impact on the community becomes increasingly pronounced. A couple invested in building a legacy of love becomes a microcosm of positive change within the larger society. Their actions, infused with intention and authenticity, contribute to the exemplifying values that underpin enduring relationships.

Consider a couple actively engaged in community service, their collaborative efforts fueled by the same principles that strengthen their relationship. The positivity generated within their partnership spills over into community initiatives, inspiring others to join hands in creating a more compassionate and connected society.

In navigating the intricacies of a relationship, couples wield profound agency—the power to initiate waves of positivity that extend far beyond their immediate connection. The ripple effect, born out of intentional love, becomes a testament to the transformative influence of enduring and committed partnerships.

Considering this perspective, our instructions become as clear as a garment tag. Just as a tag might indicate a machine wash with light colors, clarifying the washing process, our battle instructions are explicit: be strong, be creative, endure, and resist. Endure doesn't imply a standoff or an aggressive attack; instead, the directive is to stand firm and oppose adversity.

After the battle, the goal is for you to remain standing firm. If you adhere to the instructions and care for each other as directed, the marital foundation will endure despite the storms. There are moments when our perspective may lead us to believe that our challenges have inflicted irreparable damage. However, it's crucial not to succumb to such misconceptions.

In one of my favorite scenes from The Wizard of Oz, Dorothy, and her companions embark on perilous journeys only to discover the wizard is a fraud. Similarly, our adversary tries to divert our attention from the Lord's words, urging us to ignore the Creator who made us, is never wrong, and loves us more than we can comprehend. The distraction aims to obscure our seed potential. Instead of getting swayed, discern the source of the distraction, often revealing the areas where God intends to bless you—the opposite of the enemy's primary attacks.

Stand your ground by putting on the belt of truth and the body armor of God's righteousness. Honest assessment is the only way to produce a winning strategy. A seed without water will not grow, regardless of what you say.

Equip yourself with the shoes of peace that stem from the Good News to ensure full readiness. Additionally, raise the shield of faith to intercept the devil's fiery arrows. In our marital journey, we embrace a shared mission. We recognize that the purpose of our marriage goes beyond ourselves; it is the proclamation of the Good News, the belief that God will work wonders through us.

Looking back on our first date, I remember a mix of awkwardness and excitement. I remember my date's impeccable attire—a peach shirt, blue jeans, and calf boots—while the details of my outfit escaped me. Despite a hand injury from a rollerblading mishap, canceling the date was not an option. After all, I only needed one hand to drive.

When I picked her up, I opened the door, following the tradition of chivalry. During our meal, we discussed goals, desires, and tolerances. Having journeyed through the enriching mirror of marriage, we've gained profound insights about ourselves. For those starting the marriage journey, I stress the importance of aligning your mindset with pleasing God and your partner.

Every relationship has unique moments that define its trajectory. Whether it's the anniversary of the day they first met, the marriage celebration, the shared laughter of overcoming challenges, or the arrival of children, these milestones hold profound meaning. Acknowledging and commemorating these moments becomes a ritual of reflection—a pause to appreciate the details of the relational journey.

> *Celebrating key moments is more than a mere acknowledgment; it is a deliberate act of gratitude.*

It is an expression of the awareness that each shared experience, whether joyful or challenging, contributes to the growth and resilience of the relationship. From the first date to the golden years, each milestone represents a chapter in the love story, and celebrating them is reinforcement.

While the visible display of love and passion may not always be apparent, the foundational knowledge of this bond remains unwavering.

I wore headgear during my teenage boxing days to shield myself from potential injuries. In the boxing ring, the purpose of headgear wasn't to prevent my opponent from landing headshots but to reduce the extent of injury if a solid punch connected. It might still hurt, but the helmet assured that crucial areas, like the temple, were shielded from potentially fatal blows. Similarly, by safeguarding our minds with positive memories, we can focus on strategic approaches to navigate the challenges in our marital journey.

Most people understand why putting on physical armor is crucial in preparation for a fight. Remember that a successful relationship also has financial, spiritual, and emotional challenges. But let's think about what the writer, Paul, really wanted. This part he wrote was about building good relationships. Ephesians 5 and the start of Chapter 6 talk a lot about relationships. So, it's like the final piece in growing a solid marriage, like helping a seed grow. Seeds have a tough outer shell for protection, and the armor is like that until God makes it grow.

> *In relationships, boundaries are rules that say what's okay and what's not.*

They're like a frame that keeps the understanding between partners safe. Without boundaries, there's a risk of outside influences and people with sneaky motives messing things up. If there aren't boundaries, relationships get complicated. External forces can change how a couple works together. Clear boundaries prevent this, ensuring the relationship sticks to its essential values. When you set boundaries, you focus on keeping what makes the relationship unique and happy. You choose to control the values you share and prevent outside influences from affecting the heart of the relationship. Setting boundaries is about protecting the relationship with what matters most.

Here are ten practical tips for setting healthy boundaries in relationships:

1. **Open Communication:** Discuss and openly communicate with your partner about your needs, expectations, and concerns. Be honest and encourage your partner to do the same.

2. **Define Personal Space:** Clearly outline and respect each other's personal space. Understand the need for individual time and activities that contribute to personal well-being.

3. **Establish Mutual Consent:** Ensure mutual agreement before making decisions that affect both partners, including significant life choices, financial decisions, or routine changes.

4. **Prioritize Self-Care:** Encourage self-care for both partners. Recognize the importance of caring for your physical, emotional, or mental well-being.

5. **Set Technology Limits:** Establish boundaries for technology and social media. Agree on how much time should be spent on devices and respect each other's privacy.

6. **Discuss Social Relationships:** Openly discuss friendships and social circles. Ensure both partners are comfortable with each other's friendships and social activities.

7. **Clarify Expectations:** Communicate expectations regarding responsibilities and roles within the relationship. Expectation communication should include household chores, financial contributions, and other shared responsibilities.

8. **Define Relationship Goals:** Discuss and set shared goals for the relationship. Understand each other's aspirations and work together towards common objectives.

9. **Recognize Warning Signs:** Be attentive to warning signs of potential boundary violations. Address any

discomfort or issues promptly and seek resolution through open communication.

10. **Regularly Reevaluate:** Periodically revisit and reassess your boundaries. As circumstances change, discuss and adjust boundaries to ensure they continue to meet the needs of both partners.

Remember, healthy boundaries are dynamic and require ongoing communication and mutual understanding. Tailor these tips to your specific relationship dynamics and be flexible as you navigate different relationship stages.

CHAPTER 14: THE STRATEGY - SEED, BURY, WATER, AND GROW

I vividly recall the day I first talked to a military recruiter about enlisting. My visit to the Newark MEPS station was unique – the recruiter generously drove me home in a government vehicle with a white exterior, grey interior, plastic seats, and flooring. Despite the unconventional ride, it beat taking the bus. In our conversation, we connected like old friends. He shared details about his family, hometown, and, intriguingly, the various places he had traveled during his military career – locations unfamiliar to many young men from inner cities like mine. I played along, pretending to know these exotic places. I knew that beyond Newark's greatness, a vast world awaited exploration, and joining the U.S. Navy seemed the perfect opportunity for a global adventure, all while getting paid!

The Strategy - Seed, Bury, Water, and Grow

Petty Officer Allen, in his sharp uniform (bell bottoms and all, don't laugh!), showcased rows of ribbons and medals, each symbolizing a significant accomplishment. At that moment, I eagerly anticipated the day I'd don my uniform, earn my medals, and return home to share tales of my adventures. Being a private person, I only told my family. Luckily, I had sisters. I will leave the rest unspoken. People started asking, and I would laugh, nod, and ask, "Who told you?" Confirming what I suspected, Collette and Bernadette shared my business.

The day I arrived, I swore in and took my vow to defend the Constitution of the United States against all enemies, foreign and domestic. That day, I gave my life to serve others—what an honor! Petty Officer Allen picked me up around 7:00 a.m. I said my goodbyes to family and friends. Many came out to watch me leave in disbelief, as I hadn't confirmed my departure until just a few days left.

To most people, I didn't fit their perspective of the military type, certainly not the guy who would voluntarily sign up. But I did. I sought better. The shiny new car, tinted windows, and chrome rims – a dark blue Pontiac, clean and sharp – was a far cry from the white with grey interior government car I was used to. Petty Officer Allen

The Strategy - Seed, Bury, Water, and Grow

mentioned he came straight from home, emphasizing that as brothers now, he picked me up in his vehicle. Sold! I love cars! That was going on my list, too!

When I joined the Navy in the mid-80s, Petty Officer Allen's image was the same as in the commercials. Yes, if you recall the commercials, the Navy wasn't just a job but an adventure! There was another slight difference: the guy in the commercial had a Mustang 5.0. I needed to add that slight detail.

Once we arrived at the MEPS station, hundreds of recruits appeared waiting for the swearing-in ceremony. All the recruiters were pleasant, smiling, friendly, and cracking jokes. We had a great time! Then came the actual time when the recruiters left, and the recruits had to go into a separate area for the swearing-in ceremony. I remember parts of the swearing-in: "I agree to protect the United States Constitution against all enemies, foreign and domestic." I was READY! Nobody is ever going to disrupt our peace and get away with it!

I was secretly gung-ho. I intentionally got my haircut before enlisting so I wouldn't waste time with that once I started boot camp. Indeed, they would see I only have fuzz

The Strategy - Seed, Bury, Water, and Grow

on my head and let me pass. But things were different when I arrived in beautiful San Diego, CA, at approximately 2:00 am the next day. No, you didn't miss anything. I left home around 7:00 am and didn't arrive in San Diego until the following day, even with the time zone changes. Finally, after receiving our bedding, we all passed out in a large open room. 4:00 am came quickly, and we were unprepared for what would occur. I just got to sleep and heard many rumbling metal trash cans and lids, men with freshly pressed uniforms and ribbons screaming like they didn't see us sleeping, and banging on the metal trash cans. Things changed. I didn't expect this. I was in for the shock of my life! Everyone ate the same thing at the same time. Then, we were separated onto the tarmac into different drilling squadrons like mere livestock.

We were off once separated into squadrons and met our Company commanders. I recall Senior Chief Johnson saying, "You are in the perfect place to die!" Those words resonated deeply. Those words haunted me! The truth is, he was right. The military is the fighting arm of the government. There are various levels, roles, and ranks. Even though I was a good fighter with some martial arts talent, I boxed for my local PAL (Police Athletic League) with an anticipated future in boxing for the Navy. I could see a premature demise if I do not follow the set, proven strategies.

So, it is with relationships. Most people enter marriage with images of serenity, love, support, and endless passion. That is possible. You can have all of that and more! Marriage is like the Navy; it is an adventure that will take you to many places. And at times, you will feel like you are in a foreign land. The beauty of it all is that the Kingdom provides guidelines and instructions that will help you navigate through to destiny. But for most people, there is a marital boot camp where we must lay down all we know and learn to function as a seed in fresh soil. Not because you must, but because it will make it better.

Mutual submission is vital in a healthy marriage. It's not about one person being in charge and the other following blindly—it's about mutual respect and collaboration. Healthy mutual submission is essential for a strong and happy relationship.

When done right, mutual submission results in better decisions. It's not about one person having all the say; both partners share their thoughts and ideas, working towards choices that benefit the relationship. Submitting to hear your partner's thoughts shows your respect and value for who they are and what they contribute to the relationship. Submission improves communication and makes getting your partner's buy-in easier, enhancing marital decision-making.

Healthy submission also means having open communication. Both partners feel free to express their feelings, concerns, and opinions without fear of judgment. It's like having a safe space where honesty is valued, creating an atmosphere of trust and understanding.

Healthy submission is all about cultivating a supportive partnership. Both spouses encourage and uplift each other, recognizing that their strengths contribute to the overall strength of the marriage.

> *You are teammates and each other's biggest cheerleaders through every moment of life*

both good and bad.

In a marriage with healthy submission, each partner's contributions add value. It's not about one person's efforts overshadowing the other's; both are acknowledged and appreciated. This equality fosters a sense of partnership and shared responsibility. Healthy submission also includes flexibility and adaptability. It's an understanding that each person has unique strengths and weaknesses, and there's a willingness to adjust roles and responsibilities based on what works best for the couple at different stages of their lives.

In a marriage with healthy submission, each partner respects the differences. It's okay to have varying opinions, preferences, and approaches. Rather than trying to change each other, both partners embrace and appreciate the uniqueness they bring to the relationship.

Healthy submission is crucial for a happy and lasting marriage because it fosters an environment of mutual respect and understanding. It's not about one person being dominant; it's about both partners recognizing the strength of collaboration. When both partners work together, the marriage becomes more vigorous. In a marriage with healthy submission, there's a sense of shared joy and fulfillment, but remember that submission does not come naturally. It requires intentionality, and it's not easy!

STRATEGY: THE ART OF SUBMISSION

The concept of submission is crucial in both military and personal life. It involves mutual surrender, not to weakness but to a higher purpose. The art of submission reveals a profound strategy that fosters unity and strength.

Relationship submission often conjures images of one-sided yielding, but the art lies in its affinity. Both partners willingly choose to submit, recognizing that their collective goals surpass individual desires. It's not about dominance but where each partner acknowledges the other's strengths.

Submission becomes a powerful tool when grounded in mutual respect and love. It's not a surrender of identity but a conscious choice to prioritize the relationship's well-being over personal whims. Exploring the depth of mutual submission unveils its transformative potential, creating an environment where both partners flourish.

When I think of healthy submission, I think of a movie scene where both parties are back-to-back, fighting off anyone and anything that comes to attack the union. It's not about who's in charge; it is about who has the best vantage point and ability to

BENEFITS OF SUBMITTING TO ONE ANOTHER

While mutual submission offers immense benefits, it's essential to acknowledge the challenges that may arise. Ego, societal expectations, and ingrained notions can pose hurdles. However, the benefits far outweigh the challenges.

Mutual submission fosters a sense of equality, where both partners feel valued and understood. It builds a foundation of trust and open communication, essential elements for a thriving relationship. The challenges become growth opportunities, allowing individuals to shed preconceptions and embrace a shared journey.

REAL-LIFE EXAMPLES OF EMBRACING MUTUAL SUBMISSION

One poignant example involves a couple at a crossroads in their journey. Each partner harbors individual aspirations and dreams that, at first glance, pull them in different directions. The art of mutual submission comes to life as they navigate this juncture, realizing that true fulfillment lies in a shared path. By prioritizing the greater good of the relationship over personal ambitions, they not only embrace mutual submission but also discover a profound unity that propels them toward shared victory.

Real couples illuminate the beauty of yielding without a sense of loss. Whether choosing the movie for the night, deciding on weekend plans, or balancing career demands, these instances embody the essence of mutual submission. Through their stories, readers witness the strength embedded in these seemingly mundane choices—a strength that fortifies the foundation of their relationships.

> *Mutual submission doesn't negate individual autonomy; instead, it harmonizes personal freedom with the unity of partnership.*

Examining couples who successfully strike this balance provides a roadmap for others. These couples recognize the unique strengths each brings to the relationship, and rather than competing, they complement each other. Their stories become beacons, guiding readers to understand that mutual submission isn't about erasing individuality but enhancing it within the context of a shared journey.

Challenges are inherent in any relationship, and mutual submission becomes a potent tool for overcoming them. Highlighting couples who navigated storms by embracing mutual submission adds a layer of authenticity to the narrative. These stories showcase resilience, communication, and a shared commitment to the relationship's well-being. Through challenges, these couples found that mutual submission wasn't a compromise of strength but a source of resilience and enduring love.

The impact of mutual submission extends beyond the couple itself, creating a ripple effect in family and community dynamics. Narratives that explore how couples, through their commitment to mutual submission, contribute positively to their broader social circles offer valuable insights. These stories exemplify how the strength derived from mutual submission radiates outward, influencing the couple's journey and inspiring those around them.

Healthy submission in marriage involves working as a team, respecting, supporting, and appreciating each other. It's not about control; it's about unity and forms the basis for a thriving and fulfilling relationship.

CHAPTER 15: LICENSES AND AUTHORITY

A marriage license is the only license you can obtain without being tested and proven qualified because the government assumes you know what you're getting into. Marriages can face challenges when we forget to lay the foundation. Ephesians 5:21 says to treat each other well out of reverence for the Lord. Then, it tells wives to respect their husbands in the same way and advises husbands to love their wives selflessly, similar to how Christ loved the church. A consistent theme emerges when considering the text, emphasizing the importance of our understanding of the Lord.

How can we treat each other well without a deep understanding? Imagine trying to unlock a car door with your house key at a dealership. When buying a car, you sign papers before receiving the key, allowing access without

Licenses and Authority

causing damage. Understanding how Jesus loved the church gives us the keys to fostering healthy relationships.

I like the scripture that says the Lord took a rib from Adam (Gen. 2:22). The Bible doesn't explain how the Lord opened Adam's side but says that the Lord closed it afterward. This part has some critical things to teach us. First, Adam took a rest. Sometimes, we can't do or create things when we are tired. Resting is crucial because it refreshes our minds and bodies and allows God to work in us. Imagine how much pain Adam might have felt if he stayed awake and didn't rest. We need to rest, relax, trust God, and allow Him to bring out the best in us.

Second, we should trust God to heal our wounds. Just like He closed Adam's side, God can close the wounds in our lives. It's essential to look to God for healing and trust Him to care for the things that hurt us. There are two reasons why I didn't suggest you go back to the person who hurt you for your healing. First, they have already proven they are not the safest person to approach. Second, they are not authorized or able to heal you. It's best to seek an authority with a proven track record when wounded. Someone authorized and safe.

What makes God safe is He loves us like no other. I am not referring to the love we speak of today. The English language has one word that expresses all types of love. However, according to the ancient Greeks, there are nine types of love! With nine options on the table, it increases the likelihood that you can find a more specific word or treatment. When injured, who wouldn't want to see a specialist? Good news, there is a love called agape. Agape love is unconditional love. Agape love does not depend on any external factors, does not seek anything in return, and is the least selfish.

Ephesians 5:25 discusses agape love, a special kind of love that puts others before us, even when they've let us down. This love is similar to what we see in John 3:16 and Romans 5:8, where God's example of love towards us is about giving and caring for us, even when we mess up.

I trust my wounds to God and suggest you do so because He is authorized, capable, and unbiased. I don't know anyone else who specializes in all things. When there is an emergency, most adults in the United States know they can receive assistance for any emergency by simply dialing 911. Isn't it comforting to know that you only need to remember one person/number?

When we understand how deep agape love is, sharing that love with our wives becomes easier. For those who find it challenging, showing love is like saying, "Hey, you mean a lot to me." As the late Myles Munroe said, you can tell how much something means to you by what you're willing to give up for it. And this feeling of value (or sometimes the lack of it) is something you can sense.

Marriage isn't just about having good feelings; it's a choice you make every day. When you actively choose to love, it makes your wife feel important. If love were only about feelings, God wouldn't correct us and tell us to love even those who aren't nice to us. Correcting is about improving things, showing us that love is more about deciding to care than just how we feel.

Regardless of your religious beliefs—whether you're a Christian, follower of another faith, agnostic, or atheist—one universal truth remains: marriage should be a beautiful and fulfilling experience. Anything else might signal that something is amiss or out of its natural order, and in both cases, such suspicions are likely true.

All belief systems agree that having good, happy, and satisfying relationships is essential. Why else would anyone want to get married if it didn't promise that kind of happiness? Marriage is supposed to bring joy through a strong and close connection. For this to happen, you need to know yourself well. How can someone or something improve your life if you have yet to figure yourself out? It's like exploring your background, your experiences, and the way of life around you. These things shape how you think and what you do.

Realizing that

> *Much of what we do comes from what we've experienced, it's essential to understand our background and experiences.*

These things affect how we think and act. Being honest about your identity is crucial when picking someone to share your life with. An intelligent businessperson once said recognizing and understanding your weaknesses is the key to success. In the business world, this means hiring people who are good at things you're not so good at—finding partners who make up for what you lack. The same idea works for personal relationships. True success, whether in business or relationships, is hard to achieve without being humble and looking honestly at ourselves.

Marriage is knowing you'd rather be miserable with the individual than be happy and alone when you vow to forsake all others, which includes and begins with self-denial. Self-denial is essential for our relationships. The term may sound negative, but it's a good thing: We need to understand it better. It's not about sacrificing one's identity or needs but about willingly putting your partner's well-being first. Let's examine what self-denial means in a relationship and why it's crucial for building a solid and enduring connection.

> *Self-denial in marriage involves putting your partner's needs on the same level as yours.*

It's a conscious choice to prioritize their well-being, considering their feelings, desires, and aspirations in unison with your own. Putting your partner first creates an environment of mutual care and consideration.

Small acts of kindness and thoughtfulness become second nature in the spirit of self-denial. It's about doing things for your partner without expecting something in return. These acts, whether big or small, contribute to a nurturing atmosphere in the relationship.

Healthy self-denial involves a willingness to compromise for the greater good of the relationship. Sacrifices are sometimes necessary to maintain harmony, and this ability to find common ground fosters a sense of unity and shared decision-making.

In an earlier chapter, I shared how I ask questions about situations. This practice is not only wise but also a form of self-denial. It is self-denial because it brings humility to the possibility that my way may not be the best. It also lets your partner know that you understand that you are not the authority. No one feels loved when they are unheard.

Emotional generosity is an expression of self-denial. It's about being understanding and empathetic, acknowledging your partner's feelings even when they differ from your own. This generosity strengthens your emotional bonds.

In a relationship marked by self-denial, there is shared joy in each other's success. It's not about jealousy or rivalry but genuine happiness for your partner's achievements.

This shared celebration enhances the sense of unity and mutual support.

Self-denial requires patience and tolerance. It's about understanding that everyone has quirks and imperfections. ***Self-denial means accepting and loving your partner for who they are rather than trying to change your partner.*** Self-denial in marriage is an expression of love in action. It's a continuous choice to put your partner's needs alongside your own, creating a relationship built on mutual care, consideration, and enduring love.

CONCLUSION: PLOW

> *Plowing in relationships acknowledges that your emotional "soil" might need work.*

Just like a seed needs the right conditions to thrive, relationships need effort to blossom. They need understanding, communication, and effort, similar to the seed requiring the right environment to sprout and flourish. Your marriage's potential depends on your choices and commitments.

Your relationships hold incredible potential. With some care and attention, they can become a beautiful journey of love, companionship, and shared growth that's just as wonderful as any other. So, as you move forward together, enjoy nurturing the seed of your relationship and watch it bloom into something uniquely yours.

Conclusion: Plow

Now, what's this plowing thing all about? Think of it as getting your relationship ready for growth. Like clearing away rocks or stones before planting a seed, plowing in your relationship is about handling any obstacles or issues hindering its growth.

When you plow a field, it's not just about digging up dirt. It's about making the soil soft and welcoming for the seed. In your relationship, plowing means creating the best possible environment for growth. It's like making the ground smooth so that the roots of your relationship can easily take hold and flourish.

Plowing in relationships is like digging into your thoughts and feelings. It's about realizing that the "ground" of your emotions and understanding might be challenging or compacted. Like you'd loosen up the soil in a garden to help plants grow, plowing in relationships is about loosening up and improving your emotional landscape.

Why is this important? Well, think of it this way: plowing the emotional "soil" within yourself is like creating better air circulation for your relationship to breathe. It's ensuring there's room for nutrients – like understanding and patience – to reach your relationship. And just as water is crucial for a plant to grow, plowing allows emotions and communication to flow freely, making it easier for the seed of your relationship to take root and thrive.

Plowing in relationships acknowledges that your emotional "soil" might need work.

It's the introspective journey you take to ensure that the ground is ready for a healthy and happy relationship to grow. Remember, it's not just about having the seed; it's about making sure the place it's going into is the best it can be. So, grab that metaphorical shovel and prepare to plow the way for a strong and flourishing relationship!

Like unplowed ground, your life might be naturally compact if you are unprepared for a seed. Compacted soil is so dense that it interferes with and sometimes prohibits a seed from germinating or growing. Compacted relational soil may have all the nutrients required for a seed to germinate but lacks breathing space. As a single person, having compacted soil may be a safeguard to keep weed seeds and unwanted seeds from germinating. Compaction includes being open to learning new ways of doing something and the inability to compromise. The most

Conclusion: Plow

dangerous aspect of a relationship is the lone ranger compaction.

The lone ranger compaction is when the individual is confident that they have all they need and don't. It may be true that everything required to grow a seed is in them, but the two most important things are lacking or at least undernourished. Those things are air and seed. Air represents a life of possibilities. If the relational soil is too compact, neither air nor water can penetrate. Compacted soil requires much more water and time for the seed to get wet. Are you sure that your prospective partner will know that there is a suitable seed within you if every time they attempt to reach you, water the seed of the relationship within and see their efforts rolling off? Being too closed off restricts your ability to grow.

Categorization in the dating space refers to a person with compacted soil who is or plays hard to get. While some resistance and comparing are good for safeguarding, it is wise to assure the person you would like to be in a relationship with that there is growth potential. The struggle is whether there is safety for a single individual with compacted soil. Compacted soil is used in roadways because it can carry more weight. For a single individual, compacted soil, in some areas of life, is beneficial as it can help you withstand more weight and preserve the marriage seed within you during your season of singleness. When you find a suitable partner, plow the compacted areas for a relationship. Remember, a seed can not produce a thriving root system in compacted ground. Compacting, in this sense, conserves the resources within. It is a deliberate effort to preserve the nutrients contained in your soil.

> *While the desire for a partner is natural, leaving open space without groundwork is neither natural nor productive.*

Plowing reveals stones and rocks, inherent components of the earth. Expect them, understanding they might have been innocuous in a previous season. However, when you're ready to grow something new, the stones and rocks require removal to benefit your harvest.

Think of these stones and rocks as potential obstacles to your relationship's growth. It could be a past misunderstanding or a lingering issue. Plowing brings these things to the surface so you can see them. It's all about

Conclusion: Plow

acknowledging obstacles and that you can do something together.

Removing these emotional stones and rocks is like clearing the path for your relationship to grow freely. If you leave them, they might hinder the healthy development of your relationship "harvest." Taking them out ensures your emotional soil is smooth and obstacle-free.

It's all about being aware that there might be old issues or misunderstandings in your relationship soil. Plowing brings them up, and now you can clear the way for a more robust, healthy relationship. It's like ensuring the ground is ready and welcoming for the new seeds of understanding and love you want to plant. So, don't be surprised by the stones; just be prepared to clear them away for the benefit of your relationship.

I've saved this point for last, so it will linger as you consider the book's broader themes.

> *Remember, plowing your life and clearing the rocks and stones are your responsibility, not your partner's.*

Conclusion: Plow

While your partner may see the rocks and stones in your life- the obstacles- you can only remove them. Don't let the discomfort of seeing your challenges lead you to conceal them. Instead, remove them so you can grow closer. Your vantage point is different from your partner's, and vice versa. The discovery of a stone is beneficial—it not only aids your relationship but also allows other aspects to flourish.

As we conclude our time together, let's reflect on the seeds and fields we've plowed in your relationship's garden. We've explored the profound idea that your relationship is like a seed, filled with boundless potential waiting to unfold.

Here's what else we discussed:

- **Marriage as a Seed:** Relationships, like seeds, require proper care, nourishment, and a solid foundation to thrive. The concept of "seed sorting" emphasizes self-awareness and compatibility in forming lasting connections.

- **The Importance of Self-Discovery:** Before seeking a partner, understanding your emotional health, values, and goals is essential. Purposeful singleness allows individuals to grow, heal, and prepare for a healthy relationship.

Conclusion: Plow

- **Foundation of Shared Values**: A strong marriage is rooted in shared values, mutual respect, and a clear vision for the future. Without alignment in core beliefs, relationships may face unnecessary conflicts.
- **Intentionality in Relationships**: Building a successful marriage requires deliberate effort, including effective communication, emotional vulnerability, and shared goals.
- **The Role of Challenges**: Adversity is like rain for a seed—when navigated together, it can strengthen relationships by deepening emotional roots.
- **Humility and Growth**: A successful relationship requires humility, the willingness to acknowledge personal weaknesses, and the openness to grow alongside a partner.
- **The Power of Communication**: Open, honest, consistent communication builds intimacy and trust. Active listening and respectful conflict resolution are cornerstones of a thriving marriage.
- **Respecting Differences**: Understanding and appreciating a partner's individuality enhances

harmony. Learning their "love language" fosters connection and mutual appreciation.

- **Patience in Growth**: Building a strong relationship takes time. Just as seeds require nurturing to grow, relationships demand patience and continuous care.
- **Purposeful Dating and Marriage**: Entering relationships with intentionality ensures alignment in purpose, values, and goals, creating a partnership that supports mutual growth and fulfillment.

As you enter the next chapter of your relationship, remember that each day is an opportunity to water the seeds you planted. Cultivate the soil with communication, understanding, and a commitment to shared growth. Celebrate the blossoms of joy and weather the storms together, knowing that your nurtured roots run deep.

I encourage you to tend to your relationship garden with love and intention. Let the lessons you learn serve you well, and may the fruits of your shared efforts be a testament to the strength and beauty that can blossom when two hearts work together.

Conclusion: Plow

May your journey be filled with love, resilience, and joy as you watch something beautiful grow from your planted seeds. As this book closes, your relationship story continues.

Here's to a future filled with love, peace, and joy—a love story that grows more beautiful daily.

www.ingramcontent.com/pod-product-compliance
Lightning Source LLC
Chambersburg PA
CBHW020534030426
42337CB00013B/848